MRS. MAYBRICK'S OWN STORY

MY FIFTEEN LOST YEARS

By

FLORENCE ELIZABETH MAYBRICK

1905

COPYRIGHT 2015 BIG BYTE BOOKS

Discover more lost history from BIG BYTE BOOKS

Contents

PUBLISHER'S NOTES 1
AUTHOR'S PREFACE 3
CHAPTER ONE 8
CHAPTER TWO 20
CHAPTER THREE 25
CHAPTER FOUR 32
CHAPTER FIVE 39
CHAPTER SIX 54
CHAPTER SEVEN 63
CHAPTER EIGHT 73
CHAPTER NINE 85
CHAPTER TEN 93
PART TWO-ANALYSIS OF THE MAYBRICK CASE 99
THE BRIEF OF MESSRS. LUMLEY & LUMLEY 115
SOME IMPORTANT DEDUCTIONS 156
MRS. MAYBRICK'S OWN ANALYSIS 160
MEMORIALS FOR RESPITE OF SENTENCE 167
NEW EVIDENCE 169
JUSTICE STEPHEN'S RETIREMENT 173

PUBLISHER'S NOTES

This was one of the most sensational trials of the 19th century. An American woman, arrested, tried, convicted, and sentenced to hang for the death of her British husband. And she was innocent. How could it happen?

Florence Elizabeth Chandler was born in Mobile, Alabama in 1862 to prosperous parents and raised in a substantial mansion in Mobile. When her father died, her mother remarried Baron Adolph von Roques, a German cavalry officer. While traveling to Britain, 19 year old Florence met 42 year old British cotton dealer, James Maybrick. The two married and for a while lived in America before moving to England with their two children.

But it was not a happy marriage and there were infidelities on both sides. It nearly came to divorce—then James Maybrick was found dead. Whether the disgrace of divorce or the potential of losing her children in a custody battle was motive enough for Florence to kill is not for us to determine here. Money would not have been a motive, as her husband's fortunes were precarious.

As you'll find when reading Florence Maybrick's account below, she was convicted on ridiculous evidence. She nevertheless lost fifteen years of her life to incarceration and nearly lost her life for a crime she did not commit.

She gained a remarkable set of supporters on both sides of the Atlantic during her prison stay. Among them were two former U.S. Secretaries of State and a famous author. Most importantly in England was the support of Lord Russell, the Lord Chief Justice.

Upon returning to the U.S. after her release, she wrote this book and attempted to make a living lecturing. She never saw her children again and she died penniless on October 23, 1941.

TO

ALL THOSK FRIENDS IN AMERICA AND ENGLAND

WHO, WITH UNWWERING FAITH IN MY INNOCENCE, WORKED STEADFASTLY FOR MY FREEDOM, THIS BOOK IS GRATEFULLY DEDICATED

FLORENCE ELIZABETH MAYBRICK.

AUTHOR'S PREFACE

THE writing of this book has been to me no joyful task, as its making has been at the expense of much-needed rest and peace of mind. In returning to my dear native land after a long imprisonment,

I cherished the hope that I might as quietly as possible be permitted to take up the threads of outward existence so cruelly broken, little dreaming that trials hardly less grievous than those left behind awaited me; for no sooner had I touched these hospitable shores, when I was met by the fear-inspiring cry, "You must write a book—you must give the world an account of your sufferings"—as if one could never suffer enough. My well-meaning friends could hardly have known what they were asking in forcing upon me a mental return to the dread past. Solitary confinement in Woking Prison (as the reader may learn from these pages) was not such an elysium that one should voluntarily desire to hark back to it, nor is penal servitude in Aylesbury an Arcadian dream. While within their grim walls I did my best to exclude from thought the world without; and now that I am once again in the world (though scarcely of it), my one desire to shut out all the abhorrent things which so-called "prison life" stands for has thus far not only failed of realization, but, under conditions even more trying than the repressive prison regime (because of the free and happy life all about, which it seemed to poor me that I had some right to share), I have been compelled by force of circumstance to return to my cast-off prison shell, and live all the old heart-and-brain-crushing life over again. However, my second "trial and imprisonment," like the first, is at last drawing to a close; and I devoutly trust that I shall be now permitted to enter upon a long-coveted rest, and partake as I may of those tempered joys which my countrymen by their beautiful sympathy have so chivalrously endeavored to make possible for me.

Theoretically my imprisonment terminated on English soil, but so relentlessly have the fates pursued me that I have been in nowise free quite up to the present moment. In Rouen, France, where I sojourned at my mother's home for three weeks, I was as much in durance to my genial enemy, the ubiquitous reporter, as when the English Government held me in its inexorable grasp. Our cottage was completely invested by him, and all approaches and exits held with a persistency which, under other circumstances, might well have extorted my admiration.

Then came the ever-to-be-remembered sea voyage. I am a good sailor, and so the physical discomforts that beset so many were agreeably minimized; but I could not: throw off the feeling that I was not yet free—the limits of the ship were still all too suggestive of the narrow exercise grounds of Aylesbury prison; and, while the eye could roam without hindrance, there came upon me again and again an irresistible desire, which the rolling billows strenuously gainsaid, to make a dash for liberty.

Thereupon followed a couple of days at the Holland House, New York, with the same persistent reporter never absent. After this experience, I was taken by the kindest of friends to where nature is at her loveliest and human hearts beat in unison with their uplifting surroundings. Beautiful Cragsmoor, with its wide reaches of inspiring scenery, most appropriately the summer home of an artistic colony, is not too easy of access to mar a desire for seclusion, and a greater antithesis to prison walls than is afforded by this aerie can hardly be imagined.

Here all things that on lower planes so cruelly vex the spirit seem far away and beneath. If only no publishers—however benevolent—had entered this Eden, what a paradise it could have been to me! However, in spite of these dread taskmasters, my soul drank deeply of the elixir so bountifully held to my lips; and when in the golden autumn all the noble woods about robed themselves in such glory as may be seen nowhere outside my beloved native land—and perchance nowhere here more ravishingly than in these Hudson Valley uplands—the rapture of my heart, so long starved within the narrowest and cruelest of confines, turned adoringly to Him who has made this world so beautiful for His children's eyes.

I need hardly be at pains to say to my readers, that lessons in literary composition form no part of the disciplinary curriculum of Aylesbury; nay, the art of writing is distinctly discouraged there, as interfering with the prescribed parliamentary regime. Accordingly, when I set out to tell my pitiful little story, I was told to look at myself objectively; then to pry into myself subjectively; then to regard both in their relation to the outside world—to describe how this, that, or the other affected me; in short, as one of them, more deep in science than others, expressed it, "We want as much as possible of the psychology of your prison life."

I surreptitiously looked up that awe-inspiring word in a dictionary, and found that it refers to the soul, and that it was my soul they wanted me to lay bare. I vehemently protested that that belonged to my God, and I had no right to expose it for daws to peck at. But the publishers, with the aid of my friends, persuaded me that the public would give me their tenderest regard, and that possibly the humanities might be furthered a bit if the story of a woman—whatever might be her failings in other directions—wholly guiltless of the terrible charge of wilful murder, and for which in her innocence she was made to suffer so cruelly, be given in fullest heart detail to a sympathetic world. So I have done what I trust is best for all—spared myself as little as possible, lest the picture fail from suppression—and my dearest heart-hope is that somewhat of good may come of it, especially in behalf of those whom a dire fate shall compel to follow in my steps, with bruised spirits and bleeding feet.

Sketch of My Ancestry

I was born at Mobile, Ala., September 3, 1862. In searching for some account of my genealogy, I found a published letter of Gail Hamilton's, who was ever one of my most eloquent and steadfast champions, and to whom I owe a debt of gratitude I can never adequately express. From this it appears that I am the great-great granddaughter of Rev. Benjamin Thurston, a graduate of Harvard College, who settled at North Hampton, N. H., and of his wife, Sarah Phillips, who was the sister of John Phillips, who founded Phillips' Academy in Exeter, endowed a professorship in Dartmouth, and contributed funds to Princeton; and who was the aunt of Samuel Phillips, who founded Phillips's Academy at Andover.

The mother of Sarah Phillips was Elizabeth Green, and from her the name of Elizabeth has come down in regular descent to myself.

Elizabeth, daughter of Benjamin Thurston and Sarah Phillips, married James Milk Ingraham. Joseph H. Ingraham, of this family, gave to Portland, Me., for its improvement, property now amounting in value to millions—beautiful State Street, the market, the property of the High School, and much more. One of the Ingrahams was the wife of Philander Chase, the first Bishop of Illinois, uncle of Salmon P. Chase, who was Secretary of the Treasury under Lincoln and Chief Justice of the Supreme Court of the United States. Of the Ingraham family was that Commodore Ingraham who won laurels for his country and himself by rescuing Martin Koszata from the clutch of Austria. Connected with the Ingrahams was that Edward Preble, born at Falmouth Neck, whose father served under Wolfe and was wounded at Quebec; also that Commander Preble whose achievement before Tripoli was rewarded with a gold medal and the thanks of Congress. Rev. John Phillips and Thurston Ingraham, author 2 17 of "Why We Believe the Bible," both rectors in the Protestant Episcopal Church, were sons of James Milk Ingraham and Elizabeth Thurston Ingraham. John Ingraham, son of the preceding, is rector of Grace Church, St. Louis, Mo. His sister, Elizabeth Thurston Ingraham, married Darius Blake Holbrook, who was born in Dorchester, Mass. His mother was a Ridgeway. Her sister married a Quincy, and was aunt to John Quincy Adams. Mr. Holbrook was an originator of the land grant for the Illinois Central Railroad and its first president. He owned Cairo, at the mouth of the Ohio, and was associated with Cyrus Field in laying the first Atlantic cable. Caroline Elizabeth was the only child of Darius Blake Holbrook and Elizabeth Thurston Holbrook. She married William G. Chandler, of the banking house of St. John Powers & Co., Mobile, Ala. William G. Chandler's father was Daniel Chandler, a lawyer of high standing in Georgia; his mother was Sarah Campbell, a sister of John A. Campbell, at one time Assistant Secretary" of State for the Confederacy, and previously judge of the Supreme Court of the United States. Judge L. Q. C. Lamar, long a United States Senator, and afterward a justice of the Supreme Court, was near of kin.

To William G. Chandler and Caroline Elizabeth Holbrook Chandler two children were born—Holbrook St. John and Florence Elizabeth. Their father died in 1863, and their mother, on account of the war, took the children abroad to be educated. The son died while pursuing his medical studies.

As will be seen from the above summary of Gail Hamilton's statement, I am descended, on both my paternal and my maternal side for generations, from good American stock. I was educated partly in Europe and partly in America, under the instruction of masters and governesses. I was too delicate for college life. I lived partly with my maternal grandmother, Elizabeth Holbrook, of New York, and partly with my mother, the Baroness von Roques, whose home was abroad. When not with them I was visiting or traveling with friends. My life was much the same as that of any other girl who enjoyed the pleasures of youth with a happy heart. I was very fond of tracing intricate designs and copying the old-time churches and cathedrals. My special pastime, however, was riding, and this I could indulge in to my heart's content when residing with my stepfather, Baron Adolph von Roques, who, now retired, was at that time a cavalry officer in the Eighth Cuirassier Regiment of the German army and stationed at Cologne.

At the age of eighteen I married James Maybrick, on the 27th of July, 1881, at St. James Church, Piccadilly, London, and returned to America, where we made our home at Norfolk, Va. For business reasons we settled in a suburb of Liverpool called Aigworth. A son was born to us on the 24th of March, 1882, and a daughter on June 20, 1886.

Florence Elizabeth Maybrick.

CHAPTER ONE

Before the Trial

My Arrest

SLOWLY consciousness returned. I opened my eyes. The room was in darkness. All was still. Suddenly the silence was broken by the bang of a closing door which startled me out of my stupor. Where was I? Why was I alone? What awful thing had happened? A flash of memory! My husband was dead! I drifted once more away from the things of sense. Then a voice, as if a long way off, spoke. A feeling of pain and distress shot through my body. I opened my eyes in terror. Edwin Maybrick was bending over me as I lay upon my bed. He had my arms tightly gripped, and was shaking me violently. "I want your keys—do you hear? Where are your keys?" he exclaimed harshly. I tried to form a reply, but the words choked me, and once more I passed into unconsciousness.

It is the dawn of a Sabbath day [May 12, 1889]. I am still lying in my clothes, neglected and uncared for; without food since the morning of the day before. Consciousness came and went. During one of these interludes Michael Maybrick entered.

"Nurse," he said, "I am going up to London. Mrs. Maybrick is no longer mistress of this house. As one of the executors I forbid you to allow her to leave this room. I hold you responsible in my absence."

He then left the room. What did he mean? How dare he humble me thus in the presence of a stranger?

Toward the night of the same day I said to the nurse, "I wish to see my children." She took no notice. My voice was weak, and I thought perhaps she had not heard. "Nurse," I repeated, "I want to see my children." She walked up to my bed, and in a cold, deliberate voice replied: "You cannot see Master James and Miss Gladys. Mr. Michael Maybrick gave orders that they were to leave the house without seeing you." I fell back upon my pillow, dazed and stricken, weak, helpless, and impotent. Why was I treated thus? My brain reeled in seeking a reply to this query. At last I could bear it no longer, and my soul cried out to God to let me die. A third dreary night, and the day broke once again. I was still prostrate, the dull pain at my heart, the yearning for my little children, was becoming unbearable, but I was dumb.

Suddenly the door opened and Dr. Humphreys entered. He walked silently to my bedside, felt my pulse, and without a word left the room. A few minutes later I heard the tramp of many feet coming upstairs. They stopped at the door. The nurse advanced, and a crowd of men entered. One of them stepped to the foot of the bed and addressed me as follows:

"Mrs. Maybrick, I am superintendent of the police, and I am about to say something to you. After I have said what I intend to say, if you reply be careful how you reply, because whatever you say may be used as evidence against you. Mrs. Maybrick, you are in custody on suspicion of causing the death of your late husband, James Maybrick, on the eleventh instant." I made no reply, and the crowd passed out.

A Prisoner in My Own House

Was I going mad? Did I hear myself accused of poisoning my husband? Why did not his brothers, who said they had his confidence, tell the police what all his intimate friends knew, that he was an arsenic eater? Why was I accused—I, who had nursed him assiduously day and night until my strength gave out, who had engaged trained nurses, and advised a consultation of physicians, and had done all that lay in my power to aid in his recovery? To whom could I appeal in my extreme distress? I lay ill and confined to my bed, with two professional nurses attending me, and with a policeman stationed in my room, although there was not and could not be the slightest chance of my escaping. The officer would not permit the door to be closed day or night, and I was denied in my own house, even before the inquest, the privacy accorded to a convicted prisoner. I asked that a cablegram be sent to my lawyers in New York. Inspector Baxendale read it, and then said he did not consider it of importance and should not send it. I then implored Dr. Humphreys to ask a friendly lawyer, Mr. R. S. Cleaver, of Liverpool, to come out to see me. After some delay Mr. Cleaver obtained a permit to enter the house and undertook to represent me.

The fourth day came and went. On the fifth day, May 16, the stillness of the house was broken by the sound of hushed voices and hurryingfootsteps. "Nurse," I exclaimed, when I could no longer bear the feeling of oppression that possessed me, "is anything the matter?" She turned, and in a cold, harsh voice replied, "The funeral starts in an hour." "Whose funeral?" I asked. "Your husband's," the nurse exclaimed; "but for you he would have been buried on Tuesday." I stared at her for a moment, and then, trembling from head to foot, got out of bed and commenced with weak hands to dress myself. The nurse looked alarmed, and came forward. "Stand back!" I cried. "I will see my husband before he is taken away." She placed herself in front of me; I pushed her aside and confronted the policeman at the door. "I demand to see my husband," I exclaimed. "The law does not permit a person to be treated as guilty until she is proven so."

He hesitated, and then said, "Follow me." With tottering steps, supported by the nurse, I was led into the adjoining room. Upon the bed stood the coffin, covered with white flowers. It was already closed. I turned to the policeman and the nurse. "Leave me alone with the dead." They refused. I then knelt down at the bedside, and God in His mercy spared my reason by granting me, there and then, the first tears which many days of suffering had failed to bring. Death had wiped out the memory of many things. I was thankful to remember that I had stopped divorce proceedings, and that we had become reconciled for the children's sake. Calmed, I arose and returned to my room. I sat down near a window, still weeping. Suddenly the harsh voice of a nurse broke on my ears: "If you wish to see the last of the husband you have poisoned you had better stand up. The funeral has started." I stumbled to my feet and clutched at the window-sill, where I stood rigid and tearless until the hearse had passed, and was out of sight, and then I fainted.

When I recovered consciousness I asked why my mother had not been sent for. No answer was made, but a tardy summons was sent to her at Paris. When she arrived she came to me at once. What a meeting! She kissed me, and was speaking a few loving words in French, when the nurse interposed and said, "You must speak in

English," and the policeman joined in with "I warn you, madam, that I will write down all you say," and he produced paper and pencil. I then begged my mother to go into Liverpool to see the Messrs. Cleaver, who represented me, as they would give her all the information she required; and then I cried out in the bitterness of my heart, "Mother, they all believe me guilty, but I swear to you I am innocent." That night I had a violent attack of hysteria. Two nurses and the policeman held me down, and when my mother, outraged by his presence, wished to take his place and send him from the room, Nurse Wilson became insolent and turned her out.

At Walton Jail

The next morning, Saturday, the 18th of May, Dr. Hopper and Dr. Humphreys visited me, to ascertain whether I was in a condition to permit of formal proceedings taking place in my bedroom. In a few minutes they gave their consent. The magistrates and others then came up-stairs.

There were present Colonel Bidwell, Mr. Swift (clerk), Superintendent Bryning, and my lawyers, the Messrs. Cleaver, Dr. Hopper, and Dr. Humphreys. I was fully conscious, but too prostrate to make any movement. Besides those in the room, there were seated outside the policeman and the nurse. Superintendent Bryning, who had taken up his position at the foot of the bed, said: "This person is Mrs. Maybrick, charged with causing the death of the late James Maybrick. She is charged with causing his death by administering poison to him. I understand that her consent is given to a remand, and therefore I need not introduce nor give evidence."

Mr. Swift: "You ask for a remand for eight days?"

Mr. Arnold Cleaver: "I appear for the prisoner."

Colonel Bidwell: "Very well; I consent to a remand. That is all."

These gentlemen then departed. The police were in such a hurry to prefer the formal charge, they could not wait until the doctors should certify that I was in a fit-state to be taken to the court in the ordinary way. The nurse then told me I must get up and dress. I prayed that my children might be sent for to bid me good-by—but I was peremptorily refused. I begged to gather together some necessary personal apparel, only to meet with another refusal. I was hurried away with such unseemly haste, that even my hand-bag with my toilet articles was left behind. My mother implored to be allowed to say good-by, but was denied. She had gone up to her bedroom, so she tells me, which looked out on the front, to try and see my face as they put me in the carriage, when they turned the key and locked her in. After I had gone a policeman unlocked the door.

After a two hours' drive we arrived at Walton Jail, in the suburbs of Liverpool. I shuddered as I looked at the tall, gloomy building. A bell was ringing, and the big iron gates swung back and allowed us to pass in. I was received by the governor and immediately led away by a female warder. We crossed a small courtyard and stopped at a door which she unlocked and relocked. Then we passed down a narrow passage to a door that led into a dark, gloomy room termed the "Reception." A bench ran along each side, a bare wooden table stood in the middle, a weighing-machine by the door, with a foot measure beside it. A female warder asked me to give up any valuables in my possession. These consisted of a watch, two diamond rings, and a brooch. They were entered in a book. Then I was asked to stand upon the weighing-machine, and my weight was duly noted. These formalities completed, I was led through a building into a cell especially set apart for sick prisoners. The escort locked me in, and, utterly exhausted, stricken with a sense of horror and degradation, I sank upon the stone floor, reiterating, until consciousness left me, "Oh, my God, help me—help me!"

Alone

When I opened my eyes I was in bed and alone. I gazed around. At the bedside was a chair with a china cup containing milk, and a plate of bread upon it. The cell was bare. The light struggled in dimly through a dirty, barred window. The stillness was appalling, and I felt benumbed—a sense of terrible oppression weighed me down. If only I could hear once more the sound of a friendly voice! If only someone would tell whose diabolical mind had conceived and directed suspicion against me!

I remained in the cell three days, when my lawyer visited me. He arranged that I was to have a room especially set apart for prisoners awaiting trial who can afford to pay five shillings ($1.25 [about $35 in 2015]) weekly, for the additional comfort of a table, an arm-chair, and a wash-stand. Had I not been able to do so I should have been consigned to an ordinary prison cell, and my diet would have been the same as that of convicted prisoners. Instead, my food was sent from a hotel outside. I was locked in this room for twenty-two hours out of the twenty-four. The only time I was permitted to leave it was for chapel in the morning and an hour's exercise in the afternoon in the prison yard. The stillness, unbroken by any sound from the outside world, got on my nerves, and I wanted to scream, if only to hear my own voice. The unnatural confinement, without any one to speak to, was torture. The governor, the doctor, and the chaplain, it is true, came around every morning, but their visits were of such short duration, and so formal in their nature, that it was impossible to derive much relief from conversation with them.

The Coroner's Inquest

On the 28th of 'May the Coroner's inquest was held, but I was not well enough to attend. I was represented by my legal advisers. On the 3d of June I was still too ill to appear before the court. Mr. W. S. Barrett, as magistrate, accompanied by Mr. Swift, the clerk, held a Magisterial Court at Walton Jail. Mr. R. S. Cleaver did not attend, having consented to the police obtaining another remand for a week. Only one newspaper reporter was allowed to be present. I was accompanied to the visitors' room by a female warder, and silently took a seat at the foot of a long table. I was quite composed. Superintendent Bryning rose from his seat at the end of the room and said:

"This person, sir, is Mrs. Maybrick, who is charged with the murder of her husband, at Aigburth, on the 11th of last month. I have to ask that you remand her until Wednesday next."

Mr. Swift: "Mr. Cleaver, her solicitor, has sent me a note in which he consents to a remand until Wednesday."

Mr. Barrett: "If there is no objection she will be remanded until Wednesday morning."

A Plank for a Bed

The magistrate then signed the document authorizing the remand, and I withdrew. On the 5th of June the adjourned inquest was held, and I was taken from jail at half-past eight in the morning to the Coroner's Court in a cab, accompanied by Dr. O'Hagan, a female attendant, and a policeman. I was taken into the ante-room for the purpose of being identified by the witnesses for the prosecution. I was not taken into court, but at three o'clock Mr. Holbrook Gaskell, a magistrate, attended for the purpose of granting another remand, pending the result of the inquest, and again no evidence was given in my presence. I was taken to the county police station, Lark Lane. I passed the night in a cell which contained only a plank board as a bed. It was dark, damp, dirty, and horrible. A policeman, taking pity on me, brought me a blanket to lie on. In the adjoining cell, in a state of intoxication, two men were raving and cursing throughout the night. I had no light—there was no one to speak to. I was kept there three days, until the coroner's jury had returned their verdict. A greengrocer nearby, named Mrs. Pretty, to whom I had occasionally given orders for fruit, sent me in a daily gift of her best with a note of sympathy—a deed all the more striking in its generosity and nobleness, since the charity of none other of my own sex had reached to that degree of justice to regard me as innocent until proven guilty.

The Verdict of the Coroner's Jury

On the 6th of June I was again driven to Garston to hear the coroner's verdict. There was an elaborate array of lawyers, reporters, and witnesses, as well as many spectators.

I waited in the ante-room until the coroner's jury had summed up. The jury consisted mostly of gentlemen who at one time had been guests in my own house. Of all former friends present, there was only one who had the moral courage to approach me and shake my hand. Throughout the time I sat awaiting the call to appear before the coroner he remained beside me, speaking words of encouragement. But the others, who, without a word of evidence in my defense, had already judged and condemned me, passed by on the other side, for had they not already judged and condemned me?

When my name was called a dead hush pervaded the court, and the coroner said:

"Have you agreed upon your verdict, gentlemen?"

The Foreman: "We have."

Q. "Do you find that death resulted from the administration of an irritant poison?

A. "Unanimously."

Q. "Do you say by whom that poison was administered?"

A. "By twelve to one we decide that the poison was administered by Mrs. Maybrick."

Q. "Do you find that the poison was administered with the intent of taking life?"

A. "Twelve of us have come to that conclusion."

The Coroner: "That amounts to a verdict of murder."

Then the requisition was made out in the following terms:

"That James Maybrick, on the 11th of May, 1889, in the township of Garston, died from the effects of an irritant poison administered to him by Florence Elizabeth Maybrick, and so the jurors say: that the said Florence Elizabeth Maybrick did wilfully, feloniously, and of malice aforethought kill and murder the said James Maybrick."

I was then driven back to the Lark Lane Police Station, locked up, and remained the night. The next day I was returned to Walton Jail. How shall I describe my feelings? Mere words are utterly inadequate to do so. Not only was my sense of justice and fair play outraged, but it seemed to me a frightful danger to personal safety if the police, on the mere gossip of servants, and where a doctor had been unable to assign the cause of death, could go into a home and take an inmate into custody in the way I have shown.

On the 13th of June I was brought before the magistrates, and for the first time evidence was given in my presence. I had been driven over to the court-house the evening before, and had passed the night there in charge of a policeman's daughter, who remained in the room with me. Her father kept watch on the other side of the door. That night, on going to bed, as I knelt weary and lonely to say my prayers, I felt a hand on my shoulder and a tearful voice said, softly, "Let me hold your hand, Mrs. Maybrick, and let me say my prayers with you." A simple expression of sympathy, but it meant so much to me at such a time.

The Doctors Disagree

At half-past eight I was taken to a room adjoining the court, where, in charge of a female warder and a policeman, I awaited my call. I then passed into the court, where two magistrates, Sir William B. Forwood and Mr. W. S. Barrett, sat officially to hear the evidence. When the testimony had been given the court adjourned.

When I rose to leave the court, in order to reach the door, I had to meet face to face well-dressed women spectators at the back, and the moment I turned around these started hissing me. The presiding justice immediately shouted to the officer on duty to shut the door, while the burly figures of several policemen, who moved toward the hostile spectators, effectually put an end to the outburst. It was amid such scenes, and this sort of preparation for my ordeal, that on the following day, the 14th of June, the Magisterial Inquiry was resumed, and the evidence connected with the charge of murder gone into. On conclusion of the testimony the magistrates retired, and after a brief consultation returned into court.

Sir William Forwood: "Our opinion is that this is a case which ought to be decided by jury."

Mr. Pickford (my counsel): "If that is clearly the opinion of the Bunch I shall not occupy their time by going into the defense now, because I understand, whatever defense may be put forward, the Bench may think it right for a jury to decide."

The Chairman: "Yes, we think so."

I was then ordered to stand up and was formally charged in the usual manner.

I replied: "I reserve my defense."

Sir William Forwood made answer: "Florence Elizabeth Maybrick, it is our duty to commit you to take your trial at the ensuing Assizes for wilful murder of the late James Maybrick."

I was then remanded into custody.

I found it difficult to understand why these magistrates committed me to trial for murder on that evidence. There was certainly not sufficient evidence that the cause of death was arsenic. The doctors could not say so. No arsenic had been found by the analyst in the stomach, the appearance of which at the post-mortem, Dr. Humphreys said, was "consistent" with either poisoning or ordinary congestion of the stomach; but, after examination, a minute quantity of arsenic, certainly not enough to cause death, was detected in the liver, the appearance of which, Dr. Humphreys said, showed no evidence of any irritant poison. On this point Dr. Carter agreed with Dr. Humphreys, "but in a more positive manner," while Dr. Barron did not exactly agree with Dr. Carter.

The analyst had found both arsenic and "traces" of arsenic, in some bottles and things which had been found in the house after death, as to which, where they came from, or who had put them there, no one had any knowledge. This is the evidence upon which I was committed. Justice Stephen, in addressing the grand jury, even thus early showed a predisposition against me, due at this time, no doubt, to the sensational reports in the press. A true bill was found, and I was brought to trial before him on the 31st of July.

Letters from Walton Jail

The six weeks intervening before my trial were very terrible. The mental strain was incessant, and I suffered much from insomnia. The stress and confinement were telling on my health, as was the separation from my children. I insert here two extracts from letters, written by me, from Walton Jail. One is to my mother, dated the 21st of July, 1889, a few days before my trial:

"I am not feeling very well. This fearful strain and the necessity for continued self-control is beginning to tell upon me. But I am not in the least afraid. I shall show composure, dignity and fortitude to the last."

The following is an extract from a letter I wrote to a friend on June 27, before my trial on July 31:

"I have made my peace with God. I have forgiven unreservedly all those who have ruined and forsaken me. To-morrow I partake of the Holy Communion with a clear conscience, and I place my faith in God's mercy.

"God give me strength is my constant prayer. I feel so lonely—as if every hand were against me. To think that for three or four days I must be unveiled before all those uncharitable eyes. You cannot think how awful it appears to me. So far the ordeal has been all anticipation; then it will be stern reality—which always braces the nerves and courage.

"I have seen in the Liverpool Post the judge's address on the prosecution to the jury, and it is enough to appall the stoutest heart. I hear the police are untiring and getting up the case against me regardless of expense.

"Pray for me, my friend, for the darkest days of my life are now to be lived through. I trust in God's justice, whatever I may be in the sight of man."

Lord Russell's Opinion

I received many visits from my lawyers, the Messrs. Cleaver, and just before the trial one from my leading counsel, Sir

Charles Russell, later Lord Russell of Killowen, Lord Chief Justice of England. "The following statement made by him relative to this visit may interest my readers:

"I will make no public statement of what my personal belief is as to Mrs. Maybrick's guilt or innocence, but I will tell you, who have stood by her all these years, that, perplexed with the instructions in the brief, I took what was an unusual step: I went to see her in prison before her trial, and questioned her there to the best of my ability for the purpose of getting the truth out of her. During the whole seven days of her trial I made careful observation of her demeanor, and since her imprisonment I have availed myself of my judicial right to visit her at Aylesbury Prison; and, making the best use of such opportunities of arriving at a just conclusion about her own self-consciousness, I decided in my own mind that it never for a moment entered her mind to do any bodily injury to her husband. On the last occasion that I saw her I told her so, as I felt it would and did give the poor woman some comfort."

The Public Condemns Me Unheard

The day preceding my trial found me calm in spirit, and in a measure prepared for the awful ordeal before me. Up to that time I had shown a composure that astonished every one. Indeed, some went so far as to say I was without feeling. Perhaps I was toward their kind. I would have responded to sympathy, but never to distrust. At that time I was suspected by all—or, rather, people were not sufficiently just to content themselves with suspicions; they condemned me outright, and, unheard, struck at a weak, defenseless woman; and this upon what is now generally admitted to have been insufficient evidence to sustain the indictment.

CHAPTER TWO

The Trial

The Injustice of Trying the Case at Liverpool

MY trial was set for the 31st of July in St. George's Hall, Liverpool. Immediately after nine o'clock on that day, the part of the building which is open to the general public was filled by a well-dressed audience, including many of my one-time friends. During all the days of my trial, I am told, Liverpool society fought for tickets. Ladies were attired as for a matinee, and some brought their luncheons that they might retain their seats. Many of them carried opera-glasses, which they did not hesitate to level at me. The Earl of Sefton occupied a seat on the bench with the judge, and among the audience were many public and city men and judicial Liverpool officers. The press had for two months supplied nourishment in the form of the most sensational stories about me, to feed the morbid appetite of the public. The excitement ran so high that the Liverpool crowds even hissed me as I was driven through the streets. It was a mockery of justice to hold such a trial in such a place as Liverpool, at such a time, by a common jury; and it was a mockery of common sense to expect that any Liverpool common jury could, when they got into the jury-box, dismiss from their minds all they had heard and seen. In a letter which I wrote to my mother, when in Walton Jail, on the 28th of June, about a month before the trial, I said: "I sincerely hope Messrs. Cleaver will arrange for my trial to take place in London. I shall receive an impartial verdict there, which I cannot expect from a jury in Liverpool, whose minds will virtually be made up before any evidence is heard." Owing, however, to a lack of funds this hope was not realized.

I was at this time alone, utterly forsaken, and the only persons to whom I could look for protection and advice were my lawyers, Messrs. Cleaver.

At half-past eight on the morning of my trial, a black van was driven up to the side door, in the fore part of which were already confined the male prisoners awaiting trial. I was placed in the rear, a female warder stepped in, the door was shut, and I felt as if I were already buried. A crowd witnessed my departure from Walton Jail, and a larger one was assembled outside St. George's Hall. But I was conducted into the building without attracting attention.

At ten o'clock I heard a blast of trumpets that heralded the judge's entrance into court. Shortly after my name was called, and, accompanied by a male and a female warder, I ascended slowly the stone staircase from the cells leading to the dock. I was calm and collected in manner, although aware of the gravity of my position. But the consciousness of innocence, and a strong faith in Divine support, made me confident that strength would be given to endure the awful ordeal before me.

In reply to the Clerk of Arraigns, who read the charge against me of "feloniously and wilfully murdering my husband, James Maybrick," I answered "Not guilty." It is customary in criminal courts in England to compel a prisoner to stand in the dock during the whole trial, but I was provided with a seat by recommendation of the prison doctor, as I suffered from attacks of faintness, though against this humane departure a great public outcry was raised.

The counsel engaged in the case were Mr. Addison, O.C., M.P. (now judge at the Southwark County Court), Mr. McConnell, and Mr. Swift, for the prosecution; Sir Charles Russell, assisted by Mr. Pickford and Messrs. Cleaver, for the defense.

An Unexpected Verdict

When the trial began there was a strong feeling against me, but as it proceeded, and the fact was made clear that Mr. Maybrick had long been addicted to taking large quantities of arsenic, coupled with the evidence, to quote Sir Charles Russell, (1) that there was no proof of arsenical poisoning, (2) that there was no proof that arsenic was administered to him by me, the prejudice against me gradually changed, until, at the close of the trial, there was a complete revulsion of sentiment, and my acquittal was confidently expected.

When the jury retired to consider their verdict I was taken below, and here my solicitor came to speak to me; but the tension of mind was so great I do not recall one word that he said.

After what seemed to me an age, but was in reality only thirty-eight minutes, the jury returned into court and took their places in the jury-box. I was recalled to the dock. When I stood up to hear the verdict I had an intuition that it was unfavorable. Every one looked away from me, and there was a stillness in court that could be felt. Then the Clerk of Arraigns arose and said:

"Have you agreed upon the verdict, gentlemen?"

"We have."

"And do you find the prisoner guilty of the murder of James Maybrick or not guilty?"

The Foreman: "Guilty."

A prolonged "Ah!" strangely like the sighing of wind through a forest, sounded through the court. I reeled as if struck a blow and sank upon a chair. The Clerk of Arraigns then turned to me and said: "Florence Elizabeth Maybrick, you have been found guilty of wilful murder. Have you anything to say why the court should not pronounce sentence upon you according to the law?"

I arose, and with a prayer for strength, I clasped the rail of the dock in front of me, and said in a low voice, but with firmness: "My lord, everything has been against me; I am not guilty of this crime."

The Judge's Sentence

These were the last words which the law permitted me to speak. Mr. Justice Stephen then assumed the full dress of the criminal judge—the black cap—and pronounced the sentence of the court in these words:

"Prisoner at the bar, I am no longer able to treat you as being innocent of the dreadful crime laid to your charge. You have been convicted by a jury of this city, after a lengthy and most painful investigation, followed by a defense which was in every respect worthy of the man. The jury has convicted you, and the law leaves me no discretion, and I must pass the sentence of the law:

"The court doth order you to be taken from hence to the place from whence you came, and from thence to the place of execution, and that you be hanged by the neck until you are dead, and that your body be afterward buried within the precincts of the prison in which you shall be confined after your conviction. And may the Lord have mercy upon your soul!"

Utterly stunned I was removed from the court to Walton Jail, there to be confined until this sentence of the law should be carried into effect.

The mob, as the Liverpool public was styled by the press, before they had heard or read a word of the defense had hissed me when I entered the court; and now, that they had heard or read the evidence, cheered me as I drove away in the prison van, and hissed and hooted the judge, who with difficulty gained his carriage.

In the Shadow of Death

In all the larger local English prisons there is one room, swept and ready, the sight of which cannot fail to stir unwonted thoughts. The room is large, with barred windows, and contains only a bed and a chair. It is the last shelter of those whom the law declares to have forfeited their lives. Near by is a small brick building in the prison-yard, that has apparently nothing to connect it with the room; yet they are joined by a sinister suggestion.

For nearly three terrible weeks I was confined in this cell of the condemned, to taste the bitterness of death under its most appalling and shameful aspect. I was carefully guarded by two female warders, who would gladly have been spared the task. They might not read nor sleep; at my meals, through my prayers, during every moment of agony, they still watched on and rarely spoke. Many have asked me what my feelings were at that awful time. I remember little in the way of details as to my state of mind. I was too overwhelmed for either analytic or collective thought. Conscious of my innocence, I had no fear of physical death, for the love of my Heavenly Father was so enveloping that death seemed to me a blessed escape from a world in which such an unspeakable travesty of justice could take place; while I petitioned for a reconsideration of the verdict, it was wholly for the sake of my mother and my children.

I knew nothing of any public efforts for my relief. I was held fast on the wheels of a slow-moving machine, hypnotized by the striking hours and the flight of my numbered minutes, with the gallows staring me in the face. The date of my execution was not told me at Walton Jail, but I heard afterward that it was to have taken place on the 26th of August. On the 22d, while I was taking my daily exercise in the yard attached to the condemned cell, the governor, Captain Anderson, accompanied by the chief matron, entered. He called me to him, and, with a voice which—all honor to him—trembled with emotion, said:

"Maybrick, no commutation of sentence has come down to-day, and I consider it my duty to tell you to prepare for death."

"Thank you, governor," I replied; "my conscience is clear. God's will be done."

Commutation of Sentence

He then walked away and I returned to my cell. The female warder was weeping silently, but I was calm and spent the early part of the night in my usual prayers. About midnight exhausted nature could bear no more, and I fainted. I had barely regained consciousness when I heard the shuffle of feet outside, the click of the key in the lock—that warning catch in the slow machinery of my doom. I sprang up, and with one supreme effort of will braced myself for what I believed was the last act of my life. The governor and a chaplain entered, followed by a warder. They read my expectation in my face, and the governor, hastening forward, exclaimed in an agitated voice: "It is well; it is good news!" When I opened my eyes once more I was lying in bed in the hospital, and I remained there until I was taken to Woking Convict Prison.

CHAPTER THREE

In Solitary Confinement

Removal to Woking Prison

I was hastily awakened by a female warder, who said that orders had come down from the Home Office for my removal that day to a convict prison.

When I left, the governor was standing at the gate, and, with a kindliness of voice which I deeply appreciated, told me to be brave and good.

A crowd was in waiting at the station. I was roughly hustled through it into a third-class carriage.

The only ray of light that penetrated those dark hours of my journey came from an American woman. God bless her, whoever she is or wherever she is! At every station that the train stopped she got out and came to the carriage door and spoke words of sympathy and comfort. She was the first of my countrywomen to voice to me the protest that swelled into greater volume as the years rolled by.

As the train drew up at Woking station a crowd assembled. Outside stood a cab, to which I was at once conducted, and we drove through lovely woods; the scent of flowers was wafted by the breeze into what seemed to be a hearse that was bearing me on toward my living tomb.

As we approached the prison the great iron gate swung wide, and the cab drove silently into the yard. There I descended. The governor gave an order, and a woman —who I afterward found was assistant superintendent—came forward. Accompanied by her and an officer, I was led across a near-by yard to a building which stood somewhat apart from the others and is known as the infirmary. There a principal matron received me, and the assistant superintendent and the chief matron returned to their quarters.

The Convict Uniform

In the grasp of what seemed to me a horrible nightmare, I found myself in a cell with barred windows, a bed, and a chair. Without, the stillness of death reigned. I remained there perhaps half an hour when the door opened and I was commanded by a female warder to follow her. In a daze I obeyed mechanically. We crossed the same yard again and entered a door that led into a room containing only a fireplace, a table, and a bath. Here I was told to take off my clothes, as those I had traveled in had to be sent back to the prison at Liverpool, where they belonged.

When I was dressed in the uniform to which the greatest stigma and disgrace is attached, I was told to sit down. The warder then stepped quickly forward, and with a pair of scissors cut off my hair to the nape of my neck. This act seemed, above all others, to bring me to a sense of my degradation, my litter helplessness; and the iron of the awful tragedy, of which I was the innocent victim, entered my soul. I was then weighed and my height taken. My weight was one hundred and twelve pounds, and my height five feet three inches.

Once more I was bidden to "follow my guide. We recrossed the yard and entered the infirmary. Mere I was locked in the cell already mentioned. At last I could be alone after the anguish and torture of the day. I prayed for sleep that I might lose consciousness of my intolerable anguish. But sleep, that gentle nurse of the sad and suffering, came not. What a night! I shudder even now at the memory of it. Physically exhausted, smarting with the thought of the cruel, heartless way in which I had been beaten down and trodden under foot, I felt that mortal death would have been more merciful than the living death to which I was condemned. In the adjoining cell an insane woman was raving and weeping throughout the night, and I wondered whether in the years to come I should become like her.

The next day I was visited by the governor on his official rounds. Then the doctor came and made a medical examination, and ordered me to be detained in the infirmary until further orders. My mind is a blank as to what happened for some time afterward. My next remembrance is being told by a coarse-looking, harsh-spoken female warder to get ready to go into the prison. Once more I was led across the big yard, and then I stood within the walls that were to be for years my tomb. Outside the sun was shining and the birds were singing.

In Solitary Confinement

Without, picture a vast outline of frowning masonry. Within, when I had passed the double outer gates and had been locked out and locked in in succession, I found myself in a central hall, from which ran cage-like galleries divided into tiers and landings, with a row of small cells on either side. The floors are of stone, the landings of slate, the railings of steel, and the stairs of iron. Wire netting is stretched over the lowest tier to prevent prisoners from throwing themselves over in one of those frenzies of rage and despair of which every prison has its record. Within their walls can be found, above all places, that most degrading, heart-breaking product of civilization, a human automaton. All will, all initiative, all individuality, all friendship, all the things that make human beings attractive to one another, are absent. Suffering there is dumb, and when it goes beyond endurance—alas!

I followed the warder to a door, perhaps not more than two feet in width. She unlocked it and said, "Pass in." I stepped forward, but started back in horror. Through the open door I saw, by the dim light of a small window that was never cleaned, a cell seven feet by four.

"Oh, don't put me in there!" I cried. "I cannot bear it."

For answer the warder took me roughly by the shoulder, gave me a push, and shut the door. There was nothing to sit upon but the cold slate floor. I sank to my knees. I felt suffocated. It seemed that the walls were drawing nearer and nearer together, and presently the life would be crushed out of me. I sprang to my feet and beat wildly with my hands against the door. "For God's sake let me out! Let me out!" But my voice could not penetrate that massive barrier, and exhausted I sank once more to the floor. I cannot recall those nine months of solitary confinement without a feeling of horror. My cell contained only a hammock rolled up in a corner, and three shelves let into the wall—no table nor stool. For a seat I was compelled to place my bedclothes on the floor.

The Daily Routine

No one can realize the horror of solitary confinement who has not experienced it. Mere is one day's routine: It is six o clock; I arise and dress in the dark; I put up my hammock and wait for breakfast. I hear the ward officer in the gallery outside. I take a tin plate and a tin mug in my hands and stand before the cell door. Presently the door opens; a brown, whole-meal, six-ounce loaf is placed upon the plate; the tin mug is taken, and three-quarters of a pint of gruel is measured in my presence, when the mug is handed back in silence, and the door is closed and locked. After I have taken a few mouthfuls of bread I begin to scrub my cell. A bell rings and my door is again unlocked. No word is spoken, because I know exactly what to do. I leave my cell and fall into single file, three paces in the rear of my nearest fellow convict. All of us are alike in knowing what we have to do, and we march away silently to Divine service. We are criminals under punishment, and our keepers march us like dumb cattle to the worship of God. To me the twenty minutes of its duration were as an oasis in a weary desert. When it came to an end I felt comforted, and always a little more resigned to my fate. Chapel over, I returned directly to my cell, for I was in solitary confinement, and might not enjoy the privilege of working in company with my prison companions.

Work I must, but I must work alone. Needlework and knitting fall to my lot. My task for the day is handed to me, and I sit in my cell plying my needle, with the consciousness that I must not indulge in an idle moment, for an unaccomplished task means loss of marks, and loss of marks means loss of letters and visits. As chapel begins at 8:30 I am back in my cell soon after nine, and the requirement is that I shall make one shirt a day—certainly not less than five shirts a week. If I am obstinate or indolent, I shall be reported by the ward officer, and be brought to book with punishment—perhaps reduced to a diet of bread and water and total confinement in my cell for twenty-four hours. If I am faint, weak, or unwell, I may be excused the full performance of my task; but there must be no doubt of my inability. In such case it is for me to have my name entered for the prison doctor, and obtain from him the indulgence that will remit a portion of my prescribed work to three or four shirts.

However, as I am well, I work automatically, closely, and with persistence. Then comes ten o'clock, and with it the governor with his escort. He inspects each cell, and if all is not as it should be, the prisoner will hear of it. There is no friendly greeting of "Good-morning" nor parting "Goodnight" within those gloomy walls. The tone is formal and the governor says: "How are you, Maybrick? Any complaints? Do you want anything?" and then he passes on. Then I am again alone with my work and my brooding thoughts.

I never made complaints. One but adds to one's burden by finding causes for complaint. With the coming and the going of the governor the monotony returns to stagnation.

The Exercise Hour

Presently, however, the prison bell rings again. I know what the clangor means, and mechanically lay down my work. It is the hour for exercise, and I put on my bonnet and cape. One by one the cell doors of the ward are opened. One by one we come out from our cells and fall into single file. Then, with a ward officer in charge, we march into the exercise yard. We have drawn up in line, three paces apart, and this is the form in which we tramp around the yard and take our exercise. This yard is perhaps forty feet square, and there are thirty-five of us to expand in its "freedom." The inclosure is oppressively repulsive. Stone-flagged, hemmed within ugly walls, it gives one a hideous feeling of compression. It seems more like a bear-pit than an airing ground for human beings. But I forget that we are not here to have things made easy, comfortable, and pleasant for us. We are here to be punished, to be scourged for our crimes and misdeeds. Can you wonder that human nature sometimes revolts and dares even prison rigor? Human instincts may be suppressed, but not wholly crushed.

There were at Woking two yards in which flowers and green trees were visible, but it was only in after years that I was permitted to take my exercise in these yards, and then only half an hour on Sunday.

When the one hour for exercise is over, in a file as before, we tramp back to our work. Confined as we are for twenty-two hours in our narrow, gloomy cells, the exercise, dull as it is, is our only opportunity for a glimpse of the sky and for a taste of outdoor life, and affords our only relief from an otherwise almost unbearable day.

The Midday Meal

At noon the midday meal. The first sign of its approach is the sound of the fatigue party of prisoners bringing the food from the kitchen into the ward. I hear the ward officer passing with the weary group from cell to cell, and presently she will reach my door. My food is handed to me, then the door is closed and double locked. In the following two hours, having finished my meal, I can work or read. At two o'clock the fatigue party again goes on its mechanical round; the cell door is again unlocked, this time for the collection of dinner-cans. The meal of each prisoner is served out by weight, and the law allows her to claim her full quantity to the uttermost fraction of an ounce. She is even entitled to see it weighed if she fancies it falls short. Work is then resumed until five o'clock, when gruel and bread is again served, as at breakfast, with half an hour for its disposal. From that time on until seven o'clock more work, when again is heard the clang of the prison bell, and with it comes the end of our monotonous day. I take down my hammock, and once more await the opening of the door. We have learned exactly what to do. With the opening of our cells we go forward, and each places her broom outside the door. So shall it be known that we each have been visited in our cells before the locking of our doors and gates for the night. If any of us are taking medicine by the doctor's orders we now receive it. On through the ten long, weary hours of the night the night officers patrol the wards, keeping watch, and through a glass peep-hole silently inspect us in our beds to see that nothing is amiss.

The Cruelty of Solitary Confinement

Solitary confinement is by far the most cruel feature of English penal servitude. It inflicts upon the prisoner at the commencement of her sentence, when most sensitive to the horrors which prison punishment entails, the voiceless solitude, the hopeless monotony, the long vista of tomorrow, to-morrow, to-morrow stretching before her, all filled with desolation and despair. Once a prisoner has crossed the threshold of a convict prison, not only is she dead to the world, but she is expected in word and deed to lose or forget every vestige of her personality. Verily,

> The mills of the gods grind slowly,
> But they grind exceeding small,
> And woe to the wight unholy
> On whom those millstones fall.

So it is with the Penal Code which directs this vast machinery, doing its utmost with tireless, ceaseless revolutions to mold body and soul slowly, remorselessly, into the shape demanded by Act of Parliament.

CHAPTER FOUR

The Period of Probation

A Change of Cell

THE day I had completed the nine months of solitary confinement I entered upon a new stage, that of probation for nine months. I was taken from Hall G to FI all A. There were in Woking seven halls, A, 13, C, D, E, E, G, separated by two barred doors and a narrow passage. Every hall has three wards. The female warder who accompanied me locked me in my cell. I looked around with a sense of intense relief. The cell was as large again as the one I had left. The floor was of wood instead of slate. It contained a camp bedstead on which was placed a so-called mattress, consisting of a sack the length of the bed, stuffed with coir, the fiber of the coconut. There were also provided two coarse sheets, two blankets, and a red counterpane. In a corner were three iron shelves let in the wall one above the other. On the top shelf was folded a cape, and on top of this there was a small, coarse straw bonnet. The second shelf contained a tin cup, a tin plate, a wooden spoon, and a salt-cellar. The third shelf was given up to a slate, on which might be written complaints or requests to the governor; it is a punishable offense in prison to write with a pencil or on any paper not provided.

There was also a Bible, a prayer-book and hymn-book, and a book from the library. Near the door stood a log of wood upright, fastened to the floor, and this was the only seat in the cell. It was immovable, and so placed that the prisoner might always be in view of the warder. Near it, let into the wall, was a piece of deal board, which answered for a table. Through an almost opaque piece of square glass light glimmered from the hall, the only means of lighting the cell at night; facing this, high up, was a barred window admitting light from the outside.

Evils of the Silent System

The routine of my daily life was the same as during "solitary confinement." The cell door may be open, but its outer covering or gate is locked, and, although I knew there was a human creature separated from me only by a cell wall and another gate, not a whisper might I breathe. There is no rule of prison discipline so productive of trouble and disaster as the "silent system," and the tyrannous and rigorous method with which it is enforced is the cause of two-thirds of all the misconduct and disturbance that occurs in prison. The silence rule gives supreme gratification to the tyrannous officer, for on the slightest pretext she can report a woman for talking—a turn of the head, a movement of the lips is enough of an excuse for a report. And there is heavy punishment that can be indicted for this offense, both in the male and female prisons. An offender may be consigned to solitary confinement, put for three days on bread and water, or suffer the loss of a week's remission, which means a week added to her term of imprisonment—and all this for incautiously uttering a word.

Unless it be specifically intended as a means of torture, the system of solitary confinement, even for four months, the term to which it has since been reduced, can meet only with condemnation. I am convinced that, within limits, the right of speech and the interchange of thought, at least for two hours daily, even during probation, would insure better discipline than perpetual silence, which can be enforced only by a complete suppression of nature, and must result in consequent weakness of mind and ruin of temper. During the first months of her sentence a prisoner is more frequently in trouble for breach of this one rule than from all other causes. The reduction of the term of probation from nine to four months has been followed by a reduction in mental afflictions, which is proof that nothing' wholesome or good can have its growth in unnatural solitude.

The silent system has a weakening effect upon the memory. A prisoner often finds difficulty in deciding upon the pronunciation of words which she has not heard for a considerable period. I often found myself, when desirous of using unusual words, especially in French or German, pronouncing them to myself in order to fix the pronunciation in my memory. It is well to bear in mind what a small number of words the prisoner has an opportunity of using in the monotony of prison life. The same inquiries are made day after day, and the same responses given. A vocabulary of one hundred words will include all that a prisoner habitually uses.

Insanity and Nervous Breakdown of Prisoners

No defender of the silent system pretends that it wholly succeeds in preventing speech among prisoners. But be that as it may, a period of four months' solitary confinement in the case of a female, and six months' in the case of a male, and especially of a girl or youth, is surely a crime against civilization and humanity. Such a punishment is inexpressible torture to both mind and body. I speak from experience. The torture of continually enforced silence is known to produce insanity or nervous breakdown more than any other feature connected with prison discipline. Since the passing of the Act of 1898, mitigating this form of punishment, much good has been accomplished, as is proved by the diminution of insanity in prison life, the decreasing scale of prison punishment, and the lessening of the death-rate. By still further reducing this barbarous practise, or, better, by abolishing it entirely, corresponding happy results may confidently be expected. The more the prisoners are placed under conditions and amid surroundings calculated to develop a better life, the greater is the hope that the system will prove curative; but so long as prisoners are subjected to conditions which have a hardening effect at the very beginning of their prison life, there is little chance of ultimate reformation.

Need of Separate Confinement for the Weak-Minded

There are many women who hover about the borderland of insanity for months, possibly for years. They are recognized as weak-minded, and consequently they make capital out of their condition, and by the working of their distorted minds, and petty tempers, and unreasonable jealousy, add immeasurably not only to the ghastliness of the "house of sorrow," but are a sad clog on the efforts to self-betterment of their level-minded sisters in misery. Of these many try hard to make the best of what has to be gone through. Therefore, is it necessary, is it wise, is it right that such a state of things should be allowed? The weak-minded should be kept in a separate place, with their own officers to attend them. Neither the weak-minded, the epileptic, nor the consumptives were isolated.

There is great need of reform wherever this is the case. Prisoners whose behavior is different from the normal should be separated from the other prisoners, and made to serve out their sentences under specially adapted conditions.

I read in the newspapers that insanity is on the increase; this fact is clearly reflected within the prison walls. It is stated that the insane form about three per thousand of the general population. In local English prisons insanity, it is said, even after deducting those who come in insane, is seven times more prevalent than among the general population.

Reading an Insufficient Relaxation

The nervous crises do not now supervene so frequently as formerly in the case of prisoners of a brooding disposition, but the fact remains that, in spite of the slight amelioration, mental light is still excluded—that communion on which rests all human well-being. The vacuity of the solitary system, to some at least, is partially lighted by books. But what of those who cannot read, or who have not sufficient concentration of mind to profit by reading as a relaxation? There are many such, in spite of the high standard of free education that prevails at the present day. The shock of the trial, and the uprooting of a woman's domestic ties, coupled with the additional mental strain of having to start her prison career in solitary confinement, is surely neither humane, nor merciful, nor wise. These months of solitary confinement leave an ineffaceable mark. It is during the first lonely months that the seeds of bitterness and hardness of heart are sown, and it requires more than a passive resistance—nay, nothing short of an unfaltering faith and trust in an overruling Providence—to bring a prisoner safely through the ordeal. Let the sympathetic reader try to realize what it means never to feel the touch of anything soft or warm, never to see anything that is attractive—nothing but stone above, around, and beneath. The deadly chill creeps into one's bones; the bitter days of winter and the still bitterer nights were torture, for Woking Prison was not heated. My hands and feet were covered with chilblains.

My Sufferings from Cold and Insomnia

Oh, the horrors of insomnia! If one could only forget one's sufferings in sleep! During all the fifteen years of my imprisonment, insomnia was (and, alas! is still) my constant companion. Little wonder! I might fall asleep, when suddenly the whole prison is awakened by shriek upon shriek, rending the stillness of the night. I am now, perforce, fully awake. Into my ears go tearing all the shrill execrations and blasphemies, all the hideous uproars of an inferno, compounded of bangs, shrieks, and general demoniac ragings. The wild smashing of glass startles the halls. I lie in my darkened cell with palpitating heart. Like a savage beast, the woman of turmoil has torn her clothing and bedding into shreds, and now she is destroying all she can lay hands on. The ward officers are rushing about in slippered feet, the bell rings summoning the warders, who are always needed when such outbursts occur, and the woman, probably in a strait-jacket, is borne to the penal cells. Then stillness returns to the ghastly place, and with quivering nerves I may sleep—if I can.

Medical Attendance

But what if one is ill in the night? The lonely prisoner in her cell may summon aid by ringing the bell. The moment it is set in motion it causes a black iron slab to project from the outer wall of her cell in the gallery. On the slab is the prisoner's number, and the ward officer, hearing the bell, at once looks for the cell from which the call has been sent. Presently she finds it, then fetches the principal matron, and together they enter the hard, unhomelike place. If the prisoner is ill they call the doctor of the prison, and medicines and aid will be given. But sympathy is no part of their official duty, and be the warder never so tender in her own domestic circle, tenderness must not be shown toward a prisoner. The patient may be removed from her cell to the infirmary, where they will care for her medically, perhaps as well as they would in a hospital; she may even receive a few flowers from an infirmary warder whose heart comes out from its official shell; but through it all, sick though she be, she is still a prisoner under lock and key, a woman under surveillance, a woman denied communion with her kind.

Added Sufferings of the Delicately Nurtured

What words can adequately describe the long years, blank and weary enough for all prisoners, but which are indescribably so to one who has been delicately nurtured! I had enjoyed the refinements of social life; I had pitied, and tried, as far as lay in my power, to help the poor and afflicted, but I had never known anything of the barbarism, the sordid vices of low life. And I was condemned to drag out existence amid such surroundings, because twelve ignorant men had taken upon themselves to decide a question which neither the incompetent judge nor the medical witnesses could themselves determine.

So far as I can learn, there is no other instance of a woman undoubtedly innocent and of gentle birth, confined for a term of nearly fifteen years in an English convict prison. In the nature of things a delicate woman feels more acutely than a robust prisoner the rigors of prolonged captivity.

Neither confidence nor respect can be secured when punishment is excessive, for it then becomes an act of persecution, suitable only for ages of darkness. The supineness of Parliament in not establishing a court of criminal appeal fastens a dark blot upon the judicature of England, and is inconsistent with the innate love of justice and fair play of its people.

How Criminals and Imbeciles are Made

The law in prison is the same for the rich as the poor, the "Star Class" as for the ignorant, brutalized criminal. My register was "L. P. 29." These letters and numbers were worked in white cotton upon a piece of black cloth. Your sentence is indicated thus: "L." stands for penal servitude for life; "P" for the year of conviction, which in my case was the sixteenth year since the previous lettering-. This is done every twenty-five years. The "29" meant that I was the twenty-ninth convict of my year, 1889. In addition to this register I wore a red cloth star placed above it. The "Star Class," of which I was a member, consisted of women who have been convicted of one crime only, committed in a moment of weakness or despair, or under pressure which they were not strong enough to resist at the time, such as infanticide, forgery, incendiarism; and who, having been educated and respectably brought up, betray otherwise no criminal instincts or inclinations; and who, when in the world, would be distinct in character from the habitual criminal, not only from a social point of view, but in their virtues, faults, and crimes.

HOW CRIMINALS ARE MADE

There should be separate rules and privileges to meet the case of a prisoner guilty of moral lapses only, as distinguished from the habitual breaker of the laws. At present the former gets the same treatment and discipline as the habitual criminal of several convictions, and cannot claim a single privilege that the old offender has not a right to ask—for example, members of both classes are limited to the same number of letters and visits. The "Star Class" is supposed to be kept separate from ordinary prisoners. It was so at Woking Prison. But at Aylesbury Prison, to which I was transferred later, they were sandwiched between two wards of habitual criminals, with whom they came continually in contact, not only in passing to and from the workshops, fetching meals, and going to exercise, but continuously. That contamination should ensue is hardly surprising. It requires a will of iron, and nearly the spirit of a saint, not to be corrupted by the sights and sounds of a prison, even when no word is spoken. It is a serious accusation against any system to say "that it produces the thing it is designed to prevent," but such, I am convinced, is the fact as regards the manufacture of criminals and imbeciles by the present system of penalism almost the world over.

CHAPTER FIVE

The Period of Hard Labor

HAVING passed solitary confinement and probation, I entered upon the third stage, hard labor, when I was permitted to leave my cell to assist in carrying meals from the kitchen, and to sit at my door and converse with the prisoners in the adjoining cells for two hours daily—but always in the presence of an officer who controls and limits the conversation. My daily routine was now also somewhat different from that of solitary confinement and probation.

At six o'clock the bell rings to rise. Half an hour later a second bell signifies to the officers that it is time to come on duty. Each warder in charge of certain wards—there are three wards to each hall—then goes to the chief matron's office, where she receives a key wherewith to unlock the prisoners' cells. All keys are given up by the female warder before going off duty, and locked for the night in an iron safe under the charge of a male warder. When again in possession of her key she repairs to her ward, and at the order, "Unlock," she lets out the prisoners to empty their slops. This done, they are once more locked in, with the exception of three women who go down to the kitchen to fetch the cans of tea and loaves of bread which make up the prisoners' breakfast. At Woking the breakfast was of cocoa and coarse meal bread, while later, at Aylesbury, it consisted of tea and white bread. I am constrained to remark here that more consideration should be shown by the medical officer toward women who complain of being physically unfit to do heavy lifting and carrying. The can is carried by two women up two or three flights of stairs, according to the location of their ward, and the bread by one woman only. Each can contains fourteen quarts of tea, and the bread-basket holds thirty pounds or more of bread. To a woman with strong muscles it may cause no distress, but in the case of myself and others equally frail, the physical strain was far beyond our strength, and left us utterly exhausted after the task.

The breakfast was served at seven o'clock, when the officers returned to the mess-room to take theirs. At 7:30 a bell rang again, and the officers returned to their respective wards. At ten minutes to eight the order was given, "Unlock." Once more the doors were opened. Then followed the order, "Chapel," and each woman stood at her door with Bible, prayer-book, and hymn-book in hand. At the words "Pass on," they file one behind the other into the chapel, where a warder from each ward sits with her back to the altar that she may be able the better to watch those under her charge and see that they do not speak. After a service of twenty minutes the prisoners file back to their cells, place their books on the lower shelf, and with a drab cape and a white straw hat stand in readiness for the next order, "To your doors." This given, they descend into the hall and pass out to their respective places of work.

Talk with the Chaplain

Many of these women have their tender, spiritual moments. At such times they will beg for a favorite hymn to be sung at the chapel service on Sunday, and their requests are generally granted by the chaplain. He is the only friend of the prisoner, and his work is arduous and often thankless. He is the only one within the walls to whom she may turn for sympathy and advice. It may not be every woman who gladly avails herself of the enforced privilege of attending daily chapel. "Religion," as a term, is unpalatable to many. But there are very few who are not better and happier for the few moments' unofficial talk with her chaplain, be she Protestant or Roman Catholic.

It is to be regretted that his authority is so limited, and his opportunities for brightening the lives of those who walk in dark places so few. Red tape and standing orders confront him at every turn, so that even the religious training is drawn and sucked beneath the mighty wheel of the Penal Code, and there is no time for personal suasion to play more than a minor part in a convict's life.

My Work in the Kitchen

The work for first offenders, who are called the "Star Class," consists of labor in the kitchen, the mess, and the officers' quarters. Six months after I entered upon the third stage I was put to work in the kitchen. My duties were as follows: To wash ten cans, each holding four quarts; to scrub one table, twenty feet in length; two dressers, twelve feet in length; to wash five hundred dinner-tins; to clean knives; to wash a sack of potatoes; to assist in serving the dinners, and to scrub a piece of floor twenty by ten feet. Besides myself there were eight other women on hard labor in the kitchen. Our day commenced at 6 a.m., and continued until 130 p.m. A half hour at breakfast time, twenty minutes at chapel, one hour and a half after the midday meal, and half an hour after tea summed up our leisure. The work was hard and rough. The combined heat of the coppers, the stove, and the steamers was overpowering, especially on hot summer days; but I struggled on, doing this work preferably to some other, because the kitchen was the only place where the monotony of prison life was broken. It was the "show place," and all visitors looked in to see the food.

The Machine-made Menu

What dining in prison means may be judged by a perusal of the schedule as given in the Prison Commission Report:

Diet for Female Convicts

Breakfast

Three-quarters of a pint of cocoa, containing 1/2 ounce of cocoa, 2 ounces milk, ounce of molasses. Bread.

Dinner

Sunday. 4 ounces tinned pressed beef. Bread.

Monday—Mutton, Tuesday   Beef, Wednesday—Mutton, Friday— Beef.

3 ounces (cooked), with its own liquor, flavored with)A ounce onions, and thickened with bread and potatoes left on previous days, 1/8 ounce of Hour, and for every 100 convicts, 3/4 ounce of pepper. 3/4 pound potatoes. Bread.

Saturday. 1 pint soup, containing 6 ounces of shins of beef (uncooked), I ounce pearl barley, 3 ounces of fresh vegetables, including onions, and for every 100 convicts, 3/4 ounce pepper pound potatoes. Bread.

Thursday. 3/4 pound pudding, containing 1 ounce 2 drachms water. 3/4 pound potatoes. Bread.

Supper

1 pint gruel, containing 2 ounces oatmeal, ounce molasses, 2 ounces milk. Bread.

Bread per convict per week, 118 ounces.

Bread per convict each week-day, 16 ounces.

Bread per convict each Sunday, 22 ounces.

Salt per convict per day, 1/2 ounce.

Visitors to the Kitchen

During the four years I worked in the kitchen I saw many people. The Duke of Connaught,[1] Sir Evelyn Wood[2] and his staff, Lord Alverston,[3] Sir Edward du Cane, the late Lord Rothschild, and Sir Evelyn Ruggles-Brise,[4] besides judges, magistrates, authors, philanthropists and others of an inquiring turn of mind, who had obtained the necessary permit to make the tour of the prison under the escort of the governor or one or two of his satellites.

1. Prince Arthur, third son of Queen Victoria, 2. Field Marshal Sir Henry Evelyn Wood, 3. Richard Everard Webster, 1st Viscount Alverstone, 4. a British prison administrator and reformer.

These ladies and gentlemen expressed the most varied and sometimes startling opinions. I recollect on one occasion, when some visitors happened to be inspecting the kitchen during the dishing up of the hospital patients' dinner, one old gentleman of the party was quite scandalized at the sight of a juicy mutton-chop and a tempting milk pudding. He expostulated in such a way that the governor hastened to explain that it was not the ordinary prison diet, but was intended for a very sick woman. Even then this old gentleman was not satisfied, and stalked out, audibly grumbling about people living on the fat of the land and getting a better dinner than he did. I firmly believe that he left the prison under the impression that its inmates lived like pampered gourmets, and that he no longer marveled there were so many criminals when they were fed on such luxuries.

The "Homelike" Cell

On another occasion a benevolent-looking old lady, having given everything and everybody as minute an inspection as was possible, expressed herself as being charmed, remarking:

"Everything is so nice and homelike!"

I have often wondered what that good lady's home was like.

A little philosophy is useful, a saving grace, even in prison; but people have such different ways of expressing sympathy. A visitor, who I have no doubt intended to be sympathetic, noticing the letter "L" on my arm, inquired:

"How long a time have you to do?"

"I have just completed ten years," was my reply.

"Oh, well," cheerfully responded the sympathetic one, "you have done half your time, haven't you? The remaining ten years will soon slip by"; and the visitor passed on, blissfully ignorant of the sword she had unwittingly thrust into my aching heart. Even if a prisoner has little or no hope of a mitigation, it is not pleasant to have an old wound ruthlessly handled, and ten years' imprisonment as lightly spoken of as ten days might be.

The Opiate of Acquiescence

I preferred the kitchen work, although often beyond my strength, to any other that fell to a prisoner's lot, because of the glimpses into the outside world it occasionally afforded. But I never permitted myself to dwell upon the fact that at one time I had been the social equal of at least the majority of those with whom I thus came into passing contact, since to do so would have made my position by contrast so unbearable that it would have unfitted me to do the work in a spirit of submission, not to speak of the mental suffering which awakened memories would have occasioned. I soon found that both my spiritual and my mental salvation, under the repressive rules in force, depended upon unresisting acquiescence—the keeping of my sensibilities dulled as near as possible to the level of the mere animal state which the Penal Code, whether intentionally or otherwise, inevitably brings about.

  I have been frequently asked by friends, since my release, how I could possibly have endured the shut-in life under such soul-depressing influences. I have given here and there in my narrative indications of my feelings under different circumstances. Here I may state in general that I early found that thoughts of without and thoughts of within—those that haunted me of the world and those that were ever present in my surroundings—would not march together. I had to keep step with either the one or the other. The conflict between the two soon became unbearable, and I was compelled to make choice: whether I would live in the past and as much as possible exclude the prison, and take the punishment which would inevitably follow—as it had in so many cases—in an unbalanced mind; or would shut the past out altogether and coerce my thoughts within the limitations of the prison regulations. My safety lay, as I found, in compressing my thoughts to the smallest compass of mental existence, and no sooner did worldly visions or memories intrude themselves, as they necessarily would, than I immediately and resolutely shut them out as one draws the blind to exclude the light. While I thus suppressed all emotions belonging to a natural life, I nevertheless found, whenever I came accidentally in contact with visitors from the outside world, that my inner nature was attuned like the strings of a harp to the least vibration of others' emotions. The slightest unconscious inflection of the voice, whether sympathetic or otherwise, would call forth either a grateful response or an instant withdrawal into the armor of reserve which I had to adopt for my self-protection. But this exclusion of the world created a dark background which served only to intensify the light that shone upon me from realms unseen of mortal eyes. Lonely I was, yet I was never alone. But, however satisfying the spiritual communion, the human heart is so constituted that it needs must yearn for love and sympathy from its own kind, for recognition of all that is best in us, by something that is like unto it, in its experiences, feelings, emotions, and aspirations.

Visits of Prisoners' Friends

A prisoner is allowed to receive a visit from her friends at intervals of six, four, and two months, according to her stage of service. There are four stages, each of nine months' duration: first, solitary confinement; second, probation; while the third and fourth stages are not specially designated. During the first two stages the prisoner is clothed in brown, at the third stage in green, and the fourth in navy blue. Every article worn by the prisoner or in use by her is stamped with a "broad arrow," the convict's crest.

A visit may be forfeited by bad conduct or delayed through a loss of marks. When a prisoner is entitled to receive a visitor, she applies to the governor for permission to have the permit sent to the person she names; but if the police report concerning the designated visitor is unfavorable the request is not granted. When a prisoner's friends—three being the maximum—arrive at the prison gates they ring a bell. The gatekeeper views them through a grille and inquires their business. They show their permit; whereupon he notifies the chief matron, who in turn notifies the officer in charge of the prisoner.

The rule regarding visits precluded any discussion of prison affairs, or anything regarding treatment, or aught that passes within the prison walls. Had I permitted myself to break this rule the visit would have been stopped at once by the matron in charge. Consequently, all the statements on such matters reported from time to time in the press during my imprisonment, and quoted as received from my mother or friends, are shown to be pure fabrications.

My Mother's Visits

A visit! What joy or what sorrow those words express in the outside world! But in prison—the pain of it is so great that it can hardly be borne.

Whenever my mother's visit was announced, accompanied by a matron I passed into a small, oblong room. There a grilled screen confronted me; a yard or two beyond was a second barrier identical in structure, and behind it I could see the form of my mother, and sitting in the space between the grilles, thus additionally separating us, was a prison matron. No kiss; not even a clasp of the hand; no privacy sacred to mother and daughter; not a whisper could pass between us. Was not this the very depth of humiliation?

My mother crossed every two months from France to visit me. Neither heat nor cold deterred her from taking this fatiguing journey. Thus again and again she traveled a hundred miles for love of me, to cheer, comfort, and console; a hundred miles for thirty minutes!

At these visits she would tell me as best she could of the noble, unwearied efforts of my countrymen and countrywomen in my cause; of the sympathy and support of my own Government; of the earnest efforts of the different American ambassadors in my behalf. And though their efforts proved all in vain, the knowledge of their belief in my innocence, and of their sympathy comforted, cheered, and strengthened me to tread bravely the thorny path of my daily life.

Almost before we had time to compose ourselves there would come a silent sign from the mute matron in the chair—the thirty minutes had passed. "Good-by," we say, with a lingering look, and then turn our backs upon each other, she to go one way, I another; one leading out into the broad, open day, the other into the stony gloom of the prison. Do you wonder that when I went back into my lonely cell the day had become darker? I went forth to meet a crown of joy and love, only to return with a cross of sorrow; for these visits always created passionate longings for freedom, with their vivid recollections of past joys that at times were almost unbearable. No one will ever know what my mother suffered.

A Letter from Lord Russell

As the years passed the repression of the prison system developed a kind of mental numbness which rendered my life, no in a measure, more endurable. It also came as a relief to my own sufferings to take an interest in those of my fellow prisoners. Then Lord Russell of Killowen wrote me a letter [reproduced in the Introduction to Part Two] expressing his continued confidence in me, which greatly renewed my courage, while the loving messages from my friends in America kept alive my faith in human nature.

Punished for Another's Fault

By the exercise of great self-control and restraint I had maintained a perfect good-conduct record at Woking for a period of years, when an act of one of my fellow prisoners got me into grievous trouble.

It is the rule to search daily both the cell and the person of all prisoners—those at hard labor three times a day—to make sure that they have nothing concealed with which they may do themselves bodily injury.

To me it was a bitter indignity. I was never allowed to forget that, being a prisoner, even my body was not my own. It was horrible to be touched by unfriendly hands, yet I was compelled to submit—to be undressed and be searched. During the term of my imprisonment I was searched about ten thousand times, and on only one occasion was anything found contrary to regulations. I had no knowledge of it at the time, as the article had been placed surreptitiously in my cell by another prisoner to save herself from punishment.

The facts are as follows: I was working in the kitchen, when a prisoner upset some boiling water on my foot. I thought it best not to speak of it, and did not, therefore, mention it to any one. My foot, however, became inflamed and caused me great pain, and the prisoner in question, noticing that I limped, inquired what the matter was. I told her that the coarse wool of my stocking was irritating the blister on my foot. Thereupon she offered to give me some wool of a finer quality with which to knit a more comfortable pair. I was not aware at the time that this was not permitted, nor that the wool was stolen. When it neared her turn to be searched, having a lot of this worsted concealed in her bed, she made the excuse of indisposition in order to return to her cell and get rid of it. While there she transferred it from her cell to mine, its neighbor, the doors of the cells being open during working-time.

When the time came to search my cell, the wool was, of course, found, and I was at once reported. The warder took me to the penal ward, and I was shut in a cell, in which the light came but dimly through a perforated sheet of iron. This was at eight a.m. At ten o'clock I was brought before the governor for examination and judgment. I stated that the wool did not belong to me and that I was ignorant as to how it got into my cell. The governor took the officer's deposition to the effect that it was found in my cell, and reasoned that I must, therefore, have knowledge of the article. I was taken back to the punishment cell and left there for eight hours. When the officer opened the door to read to me the governor's judgment, I was found in a dead faint on the floor. With some difficulty I was restored to consciousness and was then removed to the hospital. When I had sufficiently recovered from the shock, I was allowed to return to my own cell in the hall to do my punishment. I was degraded for a month to a lower stage, with a loss of twenty-six marks, and had six days added to my original sentence.

Had this offense occurred under the more enlightened system that obtains at Aylesbury Prison at the present time, I should have been forgiven, as it was a first offense under this particular rule. The governor at Woking was a just and humane man, and he was not a little troubled to reconcile the fact of my being in possession of this worsted, when I had no means of access to the tailor shop or of coming in contact with any of the workers there who alone had the handling of it. Of course, I could not explain that the worsted had been passed into the kitchen by one of the tailoresses, who came every morning to fetch hot water for use in the tailor-room, and who was a friend of the prisoner who put it in my cell.

I was kept in the hall during the months of my penal punishment, and also for twelve months thereafter, since at that time a "report" always carried with it a loss of the privilege of working in the kitchen. When I had an opportunity, in "association time," of speaking to the prisoner who had got me into this trouble, and reproached her for the injury she had done me, she frankly confessed her deed, but excused herself by saying that she did not expect I would be punished; that she was tempted to do it because at that time her case was under consideration at the Home Office, and that she had received the promise of an early discharge if she did not have any "reports." She well knew that if this worsted had been found in her cell this promise would have been revoked. As she was a "life woman," and had served a long time, I had not the heart to deprive her of this, perhaps her only chance of freedom, through a vindication of myself. A week later I had the satisfaction of knowing that my silence had been the means of her liberation.

Forms of Punishment

The punishment of prisoners at Woking consisted of:

1. Loss of marks, termed in prison parlance, "remission on her sentence," but without confinement in the penal ward.

2. Solitary confinement for twenty-four hours in the penal ward, with loss of marks.

3. Solitary confinement, with loss of marks, on bread and water from one to three days.

4. Solitary confinement, with loss of marks, on bread and water for three days, either in a strait-jacket or "hobbles." Hobbling consists in binding the wrists and ankles of a prisoner, then strapping them together behind her back. This position causes great suffering, is barbarous, and can be enforced only by the doctor's orders.

5. To the above was sometimes added, in violent cases, shearing and blistering of the head, or confinement in the dark cell. The dark cell was underground, and consisted of four walls, a ceiling, and a floor, with double doors, in which not a ray of light penetrated. No. 5 punishment was abolished at Aylesbury, but in that prison even to give a piece of bread to a fellow prisoner is still a punishable offense.

The True Aim of Punishment

Punishment should be carried out in a humane, sympathetic spirit, and not in a dehumanizing or tyrannous manner. It should be remedial in character, and not degrading and deteriorating. It should be the aim and object of the prison system to send a prisoner back into the world capable of rehabilitating himself or herself and becoming a useful citizen. The punishment in a convict prison, within my knowledge, is carried out in an oppressive way, the delinquent is left entirely to herself to work out her own salvation, and in nine cases out of ten she works out her own destruction instead, and leaves prison hardened, rancorous, and demoralized.

The Evil of Collective Punishment

There are so many prisoners with whom complaint-making is a mania, who on every possible occasion make trivial, exaggerated, and false complaints, that it is not altogether strange that officials look with a certain skepticism on all fault-finding; hence it frequently happens that those with just grievances are discredited because of the shortcomings of the habitual grumblers. At the same time, one cannot disapprove too strongly of collective punishment which involves the utter absence of trust in any prisoner, however deserving. A prisoner slightly abuses a privilege or is guilty of some small infringement of the rules, when down comes the hammer wielded by the inexorable Penal Code, and strikes not only the one offending, but, in its expansive dealing, all the other prisoners, guilty or innocent of the offense. Many a privilege, trivial in itself and absolutely harmless, has been condemned because of its abuse by one prisoner.

I cite one instance. Each cell was provided with a nail on which, during the day, the prisoner could hang a wet towel, and, during the night, her clothes. Those who worked in the laundry came in with wet clothing every evening, which, as no change is allowed, must be either dried at night or put on wet the next morning. One prisoner pulled her nail out and purposely wounded herself. She was weak-minded, and no doubt thought to excite pity. The matter was referred to the director, Mr. Pennythorne, who gave the order that all the nails throughout the building be removed. Hence, because of the shortcomings of one weak-minded woman, all opportunity for the working women to dry their clothes was taken from them. Others besides myself appealed to the director and protested. He replied that we would be obliged to submit to the edict the same as the rest, and that no distinction could be made in our favor. Of course we could not argue the matter; the penalty fell heavier upon the laundry women and the kitchen workers than upon myself. It is a glaring instance of the great wrong done by collective punishment.

However, the prisoners had their revenge, for they never referred to him afterward except as "Mr. Pennynails."

The Evil of Constant Supervision

Individual supervision is compulsory, and in many cases it is essential, but not in all. Surely there are some prisoners who might, with good results, be trusted. The supervision is never relaxed; the prisoner is always in sight or hearing of an officer. During the day she is never trusted out of sight, and at night the watchful eye of the night officer can see her by means of a small glass fitted in the door of each cell. She may grow gray during the length of her imprisonment, but the rule of supervision is never relaxed. Try and realize what it means always to feel that you are watched. After all, these prisoners are women, some may be mothers, and it is surely the height of wickedness and folly to crush whatever remnant of humanity and self-respect even a convict woman may still have left her. These poor creatures who wear the brand of prison shame are guarded and controlled by women, but men make the rules which regulate every movement of their forlorn lives.

Some Good Points of Convict Prisons

The rules of prison, rigorous as they are, are not wholly without some consideration for the hapless beings who are condemned to suffer punishment for their sins within their gloomy walls. On the men's side the system is harsher, the life harder, and the discipline more strict and severe; and I can well believe that for a man of refinement and culture the punishment falls little short of a foretaste of inferno. But gloomy and tragic as the convict establishment is, it is a better place than the county prison, and I have heard habitual criminals avow that a convict prison is the nearest approach to a comfortable "home" in the penal world. I know that a certain type of degenerate women, after serving their sentences, have committed grave offenses with the sole object of obtaining a conviction which would send them back to penal servitude. For such the segregation system would be the most effectual remedy.

My Sickness.

I had never been a robust woman, and the hardships of prison life were breaking down my constitution. The cells at Woking were not heated. In the halls were two fireplaces and a stove, which were alight day and night; but as the solid doors of the cells were all locked, the heat could not penetrate them. Thus, while the atmosphere outside the cell might be warm, the inside was icy cold. During the hard winter frosts the water frequently froze in my cell overnight. The bed clothing was insufficient, and I suffered as much from the cold as the poorest and most miserable creature on earth. Added to this, I was compelled to go out and exercise in all kinds of weather. On rainy days I would come in with my shoes and stockings wet through, and as I possessed only one pair of shoes and one pair of stockings, I had to keep them on, wet as they were. The shoes I had to wear until worn out; the stockings until changed on the Saturday of each week, which was the only day a change of any kind of underwear could be obtained, no matter in what condition it might be. Therefore, the majority of the inmates in the winter time seldom had dry feet, if there was much rain or snow, the natural result being catarrh, influenza, bronchitis, and rheumatism, from all of which I suffered in turn.

Taken to the Infirmary

As long as the prisoner is not feverish she is treated in her own cell in the ward, her food remaining the ordinary prison dietary; but as soon as her temperature rises, as occurred in my case frequently, she is admitted as a patient to the infirmary, where she is fed according to medical prescription.

The infirmary stands a little detached from the prison grounds. It has several wards, containing from six to fifteen beds, and several cells for cases that require isolation. The beds are placed on each side of the room, and are covered with blue and white counterpanes. At the head of each is a shelf, on which stand two cups, a plate, and a diet card. In the middle of each room is a long deal table. On the walls are a few old Scriptural pictures.

The Utter Desolation of a Sick Prisoner

When a prisoner is admitted she is first weighed and then allotted a bed. Her food and medicine are given her by an officer, who places it on a chair at her bedside if she is too ill to sit at the table. The doctor makes his rounds in the morning and evening, and if the patient is seriously ill he may make a visit in the night also. The matron in charge goes through the wards at stated times to see that all is going well, but there is no nursing. The prisoner must attend to her own wants, and if too weak to do so, she must depend upon some other patient less ill than herself to assist her. To be sick in prison is a terrible experience. I felt acutely the contrast between former illnesses at home and the desolation and the indifference of the treatment under conditions afforded by a prison infirmary. To lie all day and night, perhaps day after day, and week after week, alone and in silence, without the touch of a friendly hand, the sound of a friendly voice, or a single expression of sympathy or interest! The misery and desolation of it all cannot be described. It must be experienced. I arrived at Woking ill, and I left Woking ill.

CHAPTER SIX

At Aylesbury Prison

Removal from Woking

I HAD been admitted to the infirmary suffering from a feverish cold. I had been in bed a fortnight and was feeling very weak, when, on the morning of November 4, 1896, I awoke to find the matron standing at my bedside. "Maybrick," she said, "the governor has given orders that you are to be removed to-day to Aylesbury Prison. Get up at once." Without a word of explanation she left. I had become a living rule of obedience, and so with trembling hands dressed myself. Presently I heard footsteps approaching. A female warder entered with a long, dark cloak covered with broad arrows, the insignia of the convict. I was told to put on this garment of shame. Then, supported by the warder, I crossed the big yard to the chief matron's office. There other women of the "Star Class" were waiting, handcuffed. A male warder stepped forward and told me to hold out my hands, whereupon he fastened on a pair of handcuffs and chained me to the rest of the gang. This was done by means of a chain which ran through an outer ring attached to each pair of handcuffs, thus uniting ten women in a literal chain-gang. This was to me the last straw of degradation—the parting indignity of hateful Woking; but, happily, this was a painful prelude to a more merciful regime at Aylesbury.

Some of the women were weeping, some swearing. When all were ready the prison-van drove into the yard and we filed out to the clanking of our chains. Then the door was shut and we were driven off. A special train was waiting at the station, and escorted between male warders we got in. It was bitterly cold and raining heavily, but crowds lined the road and platforms.

New Insignia of Shame

We were objects of morbid curiosity to the idle and curious people, who may or may not have felt sorry for us. But to be stared at was most distressing to all, to the first offender in particular. If the public but realized how prisoners suffer when their disgrace is thus brought to the public notice, they might feel ashamed of their lack of ordinary human consideration and pass on. But why should it be necessary at all to subject a prisoner to such humiliation and degradation? Male as well as female prisoners could be transferred from one prison to another without attracting any notice in the street or at the station, if they were provided with garments for traveling upon which the hideous 'brand of shame—the "broad arrow"—is not stamped. It is this mark of condemnation which attracts the morbid curiosity of the people. Such exhibitions and the callous disregard of a prisoner's feelings can only harden and embitter the heart and lower his or her self-respect.

Arrival at Aylesbury Prison

After a journey of nearly five hours we arrived at Aylesbury Station. The public were apparently aware that the first batch of convicts was to be transferred that day, as there were crowds at all the stations at which we stopped. When we got out at Aylesbury it was with difficulty that a passage was made for us. The prison-vans were in readiness, and we were rapidly driven away. I felt weak and faint and cold. A thick fog enveloped the town, and I could see only the dim outlines of houses appearing and disappearing as we passed along. We stopped before what appeared a gigantic structure, and then drove through two large iron gates into a small courtyard. There we descended and drew up in line to be counted by the officer, while our numbers and names were given to the governor, who stood waiting to receive us. The order "Pass on!" was called by the matron in charge, whereupon we entered a long, dark, gloomy passage, at the end of which was a strong, barred door. This was unlocked, and, when we had passed in, relocked.

I have already described what a prison is like. Again we stood in line. Then a male warder came forward. He unlocked my handcuffs and unclasped the chain which bound me to my fellow convicts. With a clang that echoed through the empty halls they fell together to the ground. My wrists were bruised and sore from the long pressure of their combined weight.

Presently the order "Pass on!" was repeated, and, led by a female warder, we went up two flights of the iron stairway to the top ward of the hall. Each prisoner was then in turn locked into a cell. Thus ended my second journey as a prisoner.

The contrast with former journeys in my life drew bitter tears from my eyes.

During the remainder of the week daily batches of prisoners continued to arrive, and on the sixth day all had been duly transferred from Woking Prison, which was then turned into military barracks.

After this short break in our prison life the same daily routine was once more taken up. Whether it was due to the change of air or other physical causes I cannot say, but from the time of my arrival I began to droop. I lost strength and suffered terribly from insomnia.

A New Prison Regime

Six months after our arrival, there came a change of authorities, and with the passing of the years a more enlightened regime was instituted by the Home Office. If a prisoner has any complaint to make or wishes to seek advice, she asks to have her name put down to see the governor.

She is then termed a "wisher," and is "seen" by him in his office in the presence of the chief matron. Her request is written down by him in her penal record, and if he cannot settle the matter out of hand it is referred to a "visiting director," to whom the prisoner is permitted to make a statement If this gentleman finds that his powers are insufficient to deal with the question, he in turn passes it on to the prison commission, and sometimes it goes even to the Secretary of State himself.

The same privilege holds good concerning medical matters. If a prisoner is feeling ill she asks the officer in charge of the ward where she is located to enter her name on the doctor's book. At ten o'clock the prisoner is sent for, and sees the doctor in the presence of an infirmary nurse. He enters her name in a book, also the prescription, both of which are copied later in the prisoner's medical record. If a prisoner is dissatisfied with the treatment she is receiving, she can make application m to see the "medical inspector," who comes to the prison every three months. But if neither the governor, nor the doctor, nor the director, nor the inspector gives satisfaction, then there is the "Board of Visitors" to inquire into the complaint.

The Board of Visitors

The idea of the "Board of Visitors" is to act as a guaranty to the public that everything is honest and above board, and that there can be no possibility of inhuman treatment. If this is the sole object in view—namely, that the prisoners shall be seen by these "visitors then the object is largely attained. They have done much to ameliorate the prisoners' condition. Whereas, at one time the women slept in their clothes, they are now provided with nightdresses; instead of sitting with their feet always on the stone floor, they are now allowed a small mat, as well as a wooden stool; and, as the result of many complaints regarding the rapid decay of teeth, toothbrushes are allowed, a concession which I much appreciated. For a short time felt slippers were granted us, but these have been discontinued on the ground of expense. The same beneficent influence also secured wide-brimmed hats for the women. Formerly they had nothing to protect their eyes, and the reflected glare from the stone walls was the cause of much weakness and inflammation.

There were several changes in the diet also. Tea was substituted for cocoa at breakfast and supper, white bread in lieu of whole-meal bread, and tinned meat replaced the dry bread and cheese previously given on Sunday.

The time of solitary confinement was reduced from nine months to four, and immediately on its expiration the probationers can now work in "association" in either the laundry or the tailor's shops where the officers' uniforms—of brown cashmere in summer and navy-blue serge in winter—are made, besides all the clothing for the prisoners' own use; also in the twine-room, where excellent spinning is done; while the prisoner with special aptitude may be recommended to the bead-room, which turns out really artistic work.

Regulations Concerning Letters and Visits

The prisoners were also allowed to receive three photographs of near relatives and to keep them in their cells. Previously these had to be returned within twenty-four hours. Best of all, the intervals between letters and visits were reduced by a month. The number of letters permitted to be sent by a prisoner varies according to the stage she is in. In the fourth stage a letter is allowed every two months, and a "special letter" occasionally, if the prisoner's conduct has been satisfactory.

The following is a copy of the prison regulations concerning communications between prisoners and their friends:

"The following regulations as to communications, by visit or letter, between prisoners and their friends, are notified for the information of their correspondents:

"The permission to write and receive letters is given to prisoners for the purpose of enabling them to keep up a connection with their respectable friends, and not that they may be kept informed of public events.

"All letters are read by the prison authorities. They must be legibly written, and not crossed. Any which are of an objectionable tendency, either to or from prisoners, or containing slang or improper expressions, will be suppressed.

"Prisoners are permitted to receive and to write a letter at intervals, which depends on the rules of the stage they attain by industry and good conduct; but matters of special importance to a prisoner may be communicated at any time by letter (prepaid) to the governor, who will inform the prisoner thereof, if expedient.

"In case of misconduct the privilege of receiving and writing a letter may be forfeited for a time.

"Money, books, postage-stamps, food, tobacco, clothes, etc., should not be sent to prisoners for their use in prison, as nothing is allowed to be received at the prison for that purpose.

"Persons attempting to clandestinely communicate with, or to introduce any article to or for prisoners, are liable to fine or imprisonment, and any prisoner concerned in such practises is liable to be severely punished.

"Prisoners' friends are sometimes applied to by unauthorized persons to send money, etc., to them privately, under pretense that they can apply it for the benefit of the prisoners, and under such fraudulent pretense such persons endeavor to obtain money for themselves. Any letter containing such an application received by the friends of a prisoner should be at once forwarded by them to the governor.

"Prisoners are allowed to receive visits from their friends, according to rules, at intervals which depend on their stage.

"When visits are clue to prisoners notification will be sent to the friends whom they desire to visit them."

While in Woking Prison, under the privilege of these rules, I wrote the following letter to the late Miss Mary A. Dodge ("Gail Hamilton")—she who was my most eloquent and steadfast champion in America:

Mary Abigail Dodge (1833–1896) was an American writer and essayist, who wrote under pseudonym "Gail Hamilton." Her writing is witty and promoted equality of education and occupation for women.—Ed. 2015

P 29, June 24, 1892.

Dear Miss Dodge:

I feel that I owe you such a debt of gratitude for the truly noble, beautiful, and womanly manner in which you have used that glorious gift of God—your genius—in the cause of a helpless and sorely afflicted sister, whose claim to your compassion was but that of a common humanity and nationality, that I feel I must send you a few lines, if only to disabuse your mind of any lingering doubts of my gratitude that my silence may have caused to arise. My dear mother has, I believe, explained to you the almost insurmountable difficulty I find in writing to friends abroad, with only one letter every two months at my disposal, and which I do not feel justified in depriving her of. I can, therefore, only express through her from time to time my heartfelt thanks for all that has been and is still being done in my behalf. I utterly despair, however, of finding words that shall convey to you even the faintest idea of the fulness of a heart completely overwhelmed by the sympathy, kindness, and generosity of my friends. My feelings of love, however, and admiration for you and them is simply beyond all power of expression.

The world may and does bemoan the gradual extinction in this generation of those finer and nobler traits of character which our forefathers so beautifully exemplified; lays at the door of a higher civilization the terrible increase of selfishness, pride, and indifference to all the higher duties of Christianity. But, I ask, where can a grander exception be found to such apparent degeneration than that displayed by the conduct of those truly noble men and women, who, without a thought of self or of the trouble involved, have stood forth to 140 plead the cause of their countrywoman? Could man do more than he is doing? Could woman do more for her nearest and dearest than the ladies of America are doing for me? No! a thousand times, no!

Some day, my health and purse permitting, I shall hope to tell them face to face, if mere words can tell, how greatly their faithful, unwearying efforts, their undaunted energy, their sympathy and kindness and generosity have helped me to rise above the depressing influences of the injustice I am suffering under, to endure patiently, to bear bravely the hardships of this life, and to feel through all that the hope and comfort afforded me by their help is but a beautiful example of the way in which God answers the prayers of his people.

I would now fain beg of you, dear friend, to express my deepest and most heartfelt gratitude to President Harrison, Mr. Blaine, and the other members of the Cabinet. Also to all the distinguished gentlemen who so generously attached their signatures to the splendid petition sent lately from Washington to the Hon. Henry Matthews,

Secretary of State, London, and to assure them of my great appreciation of the honor and justice they have done me in thus espousing my cause. Oh, how wretchedly I have expressed what I really feel and would like to say! But you, too, have a woman's heart, and you can therefore realize the feelings I find it so hard to express. It would be a still more hopeless task to try to tell you what I think of you—noblest and truest of women; that must wait until we meet. Until that glad day, believe me, Yours gratefully and sincerely,

Florence E. Maybrick.

P.S. My next date for receiving letters is 19th July.

To Miss Dodge,

Washington, D. C., U. S. A.

A Visit from Lord Russell

I was sitting in my cell one day feeling very weak and ill. I was recovering from an attack of influenza, and the cold comfort of my surroundings increased the physical and mental depression which accompanies this complaint. I wondered vaguely why my life was spared, why I was permitted to suffer this terrible injustice, when my sad thoughts were distracted by the sounds of approaching voices. I arose from my seat—which is a compulsory attitude of submission when an authority approaches a prisoner—and stood waiting for I knew not what. Presently I heard the tones of a voice which I can never forget while memory lasts, though that voice is now hushed in death; a voice which, through the darkest days of my life, ever spoke words of trust, comfort, and encouragement. Surely I must be dreaming, I thought, or my mind is growing weak and I am becoming fanciful; for how should this voice reach me within these prison walls? I looked up, startled, and once more thought my mind was wandering, for there stood the noblest, truest friend that woman ever had: the champion of the weak and the oppressed; the brave upholder of justice and law in the face of prejudice and public hostility—Lord Russell of Killowen, Lord Chief Justice of England.* He stepped into my cell with a kindly smile on his face, and sat down on my stool, while the governor waited outside. He talked to me for half an hour, and I can never forget the beauty and grandeur of that presence. As he rose to leave he turned toward me, and, seeing unshed tears in my eyes, he took my hand in his, and in his strong, emphatic way said: "Be brave, be strong; I believe you to be an innocent woman. I have done and will continue to do all I can for you."

*(1832—1900), not to be confused with Lord of Appeal in Ordinary.— Ed. 2015

It has been denied in England that Lord Russell took any interest in me other than he might in any client he was paid to defend; but the letter which I have already given, written to me at Woking, as well as various statements made by him, and quoted elsewhere, must set that aspersion at rest.

CHAPTER SEVEN

A Petition for Release

Denied by the Secretary of State

I HAD been at Aylesbury about eight months when I petitioned the Secretary of State for a reconsideration of my case, with a view to my release. To this I received the usual official reply, "Not sufficient grounds."

A prisoner may petition the Secretary of State every three months. In my opinion, the privilege of petitioning on a case should be reduced from four times a year to once a year, with the provision that if anything of importance to a prisoner transpires within that period it may be duly submitted to the Secretary of State on recommendation of the governor or director; that all complaints regarding food, treatment, or medical attention should be referred to the visiting director in the first instance, instead of the Secretary of State, who under the present system passes it back to the directors for the necessary investigation. This would do away with the continual daily distress and irritation and disappointment created in the prison on receipt of unfavorable replies from the Home Office. A prisoner petitions. A private inquiry is held, to which the prisoner is not a party, and of which she has no information, nor does she receive any during its progress or after its conclusion, save that the result, which is nearly always negative, is communicated to her. In this inquiry any one who is opposed to the prisoner may seek to influence the official mind. I will state a case in point. A friend asked the Secretary of State for the United States, the Hon. John Hay, to interest himself in my case. Mr. Hay replied that he had been informed by the Home Office that I had been "a disobedient and troublesome prisoner."

Report of My Misconduct Refuted

When I was told this at a visit I had my name entered to see the governor. I insisted that the governor should inform me when, and after what breach of the rules, such a report had been sent to the Home Office. After carefully looking through my penal record he could find no entry to that effect, and concluded by saying that I must have been misinformed. He said that my conduct was good, and that he had never made any report to the contrary. Obviously, therefore, this report from the Home Office to Mr. Hay was due to an adverse influence, of which I have still no knowledge. Statements are made against a prisoner, of the nature of which she is entirely ignorant. Being ignorant, she has no way of refuting them. Worse still, they are retained in the Home Office to her dying day, and the unfortunate woman knows nothing of them or their effect. The only thing certain is that she is further condemned.

Need of a Court of Criminal Appeal

The Home Office, while exercising a private function of reconsideration grounded on the royal prerogative of mercy, emphatically disclaims being a court of appeal or a judicial tribunal in any sense of the word. Yet the consideration of a convict's case rests alone with the Secretary of State. It is a matter of unwritten law that the Home Secretary shall act individually and solely upon his own responsibility, and none of his colleagues are to assume or take part therein.

There are numerous instances where judges, witnesses, and juries have gone wrong. Indeed, it will be found that even in cases which have seemed the clearest and least complicated in the trial grievous mistakes have been made. But in England the blame rests on the public and the bar in that no means are provided to set the wrong right. What a difference it would have made in my life if I had been granted a second trial! I could have called other witnesses, submitted fresh evidence, and refuted false testimony. Is it not the climax of injustice that men and women, if sued for money, even for a few shillings, can appeal from court to court—even to the House of Lords, the English court of last resort; but when character, all that life holds dear, and life itself, are in jeopardy, a prisoner's fate may depend upon the incompetent construction of one man, and there is no appeal?

A hard-worked Secretary of State, whose time, night and day, is crowded with every kind of duty, correspondence, and labor, in the House of Commons or in the Home Office, has to consider a vast number of petitions, complaints, and miscarriages of justice, or too severe sentences, any one of which might require hours and sometimes days to investigate. He is assisted by several officers, but, strange to say, it is no part of their qualifications (or that of the Home Secretary himself), that they should be familiar with the criminal law or the prosecution or defense of prisoners. These permanent officials are, besides, occupied with hundreds of other matters which come before the Home Office, on which they have to guide their chief. Think of the untold sufferings of individuals and families, the shame and degradation which they would be spared, if England had a court of criminal appeal.

Historic Examples of British Injustice

The Home Office detects and corrects a larger number of erroneous verdicts than the public is aware. This arises from the secret and partial methods of remedying miscarriages of justice frequently adopted. The first object is to maintain the public belief in the infallibility of judges and juries. If an innocent person could slip out quietly, without shaking this belief, he might be permitted to do so. The Home Secretary is, in fact, a politician, who has little time to spare for the consideration of criminal cases, and furthermore must see to it that his conduct does not injure his party. Thus he is often deterred from interfering with verdicts and sentences by sheer timidity. When he affirms a sentence he can throw the greater part of the blame on others if he is afterward proved to be wrong; but when he reverses either verdict or sentence, he must take the whole responsibility upon himself. This is, I believe, the true explanation of the secret and partial reversals which are not unusual at the Home Office. The Home Secretary, as well as his subordinates, must frequently let "dare not wait upon I would."

If a crime is committed and no one is brought to justice, the police are blamed; but if a person is convicted the police are praised, without regard as to whether the right person has been convicted. Hence there is usually a strong effort to beat up evidence against the person suspected, as in my case and that of Adolf Beck (see page 155), and to keep back anything in favor of the prisoner that comes to the knowledge of the police. When an appeal is made from the verdict to the Home Secretary, the first step is to consult the very judge who is responsible, in nine cases out of ten, for the erroneous verdict. It is easy to see that, where such reference is made, the judge is liable to be biased in support of his own rulings. How much more the ends of justice would be furthered by having the case retried!

God only knows how many men and women have been innocent of the charges brought against them, and for which they have been unjustly punished. I will mention a few only of many cases on record.

A man, Hebron by name, was convicted at Manchester, of murder. He was sentenced to death, but fortunately this was commuted to penal servitude for life. After serving two years the real murderer, a man named Peace, was discovered, and Hebron was "graciously pardoned."

Another cruel case was that of John Kensall, who was convicted of murder, but, through action taken by the late Lord Chief Justice Russell, was shown to be innocent. The Home Office could not at first "see its way to interfere," and had it not been for Lord Russell's clear head and splendid generalship, by which the authorities at the Home Office were outwitted, he would not have been released so soon.

The case of the man Hay, wrongly convicted, was of a serious nature, showing that he was the victim of a conspiracy; yet had it not been for Sir William Harcourt's instituting an investigation independent of the Home Office, it is very doubtful whether Hay would have been able to establish his innocence. But he did so, and a pardon was granted him.

It looks almost as if justice in England were growing of late more than ordinarily blind. Thrice, within three years, has the Home Secretary's "pardon" been granted to men found to have been wrongfully convicted.

The average man takes it for granted that these hideous mistakes must, of necessity, be few and far between; but the criminologist knows better. He, at all events, is well aware that every year a number of innocent people are sentenced to suffer either an ignominious death upon the scaffold, or the long-drawn-out living death of penal servitude.

Many of these judicial miscarriages never come to light at all. Others are purposely glossed over by the powers that be. But occasionally one occurs of so appalling a nature that it rivets the attention and shocks the conscience of the entire civilized world, as in the case of Adolf Beck.

The Case of Adolf Beck

Adolf Beck was twice convicted for crimes committed by a man who somewhat resembled him. He served his first sentence and had been convicted for a second crime on "misrepresented identity" when his innocence was providentially established. The case is too lengthy for detailed account in these pages, and I shall content myself in giving the summing-up of Mr. George R. Sims in the pamphlet reprinted from his presentation of the case in the columns of The Daily Mail of London:

"I have told in plain words the story of a foul wrong done to an innocent man.

"I have proved beyond all question that Adolf Beck was in 1896, by the Common Sergeant, Sir Forrest Fulton, at the Old Bailey, sentenced to seven years' penal servitude for being an ex-convict named John Smith.

"I have proved that he was not found guilty of being John Smith by the jury.

"The former conviction for which Mr. Adolf Beck was sentenced and punished was not only never submitted to the jury, but they were warned by the judge that they were not to take the issue of Beck being Smith into consideration in arriving at their verdict. They were to dismiss k completely from their minds.

"I have proved that if this issue had been left for the jury to consider they must have acquitted Mr. Beck, who showed by an indisputable alibi that he could not be Smith, the man convicted in 1877.

"I have proved that this terrible mockery of justice, the conviction of an innocent man for a series of crimes that it was quite impossible he could have committed, was brought about by the action of the leading counsel for the Treasury, which action was supported by the Common Sergeant, Sir Forrest Fulton.

"I have proved that the evidence of the policeman, Eliss Spurred, which was used at the police-court to assist in getting Beck committed for trial, was kept out at the Old Bailey, where it would have insured Beck's acquittal.

"I have proved that at the police-court in 1896 Mr. Gurrin, the Treasury expert, reported that all the documents connected with the 1896 frauds were in the handwriting of John Smith of 1877.

"I have proved that at the 1896 trial at the Old Bailey Mr. Gurrin swore that, to the best of his belief, all the documents were in the disguised handwriting of Mr. Beck.

"I have proved that no one in his senses could at the trial have accepted the theory that Adolf Beck was John Smith after listening to the evidence of Major Lindholm, Gentleman of the Chamber to the King of Denmark, Col. Josiah Harris, and the Consul-General for Peru at Liverpool.

"The Common Sergeant accepted as true their evidence of a complete alibi for Mr. Beck, so far as 1877 and the years Smith was in prison were concerned, or he would, it is to be presumed, have taken measures to have those gentlemen prosecuted for committing wilful and corrupt perjury in order to defeat the ends of justice.

"I have proved that Beck, after his imprisonment, compelled the Home Office authorities to acknowledge that he was not Smith, and to admit the physical impossibility of his being Smith—Smith was a Jew, and he, Beck, was not—and that therefore, by the evidence of the Treasury witnesses, he had been wrongfully committed.

"I have proved that Beck was stripped and officially examined for body marks before his trial, in order that such marks might be compared with those on the record in the possession of the authorities as the body marks of John Smith.

"I have proved that Adolf Beck had none of the body marks of John Smith, the man in whose handwriting Mr. Gurrin had declared the incriminating documents of 1896 to be.

"I have proved that all the petitions setting forth these facts and others, which fully established Beck's innocence, met with no consideration.

"I have proved that when the frauds of 1877 and 1896 were repeated in 1904, and the incriminating documents were found to be in the handwriting of 1877, stroke for stroke, peculiarity for peculiarity, almost word for word, the fact that the authorities had admitted that Mr. Beck could not be the author of the 1877 frauds or the writer of the 1877 documents was utterly ignored, and the responsible authorities, with every proof of Mr. Beck's innocence in their possession, allowed him to be arrested, charged, tried, and convicted again.

"I have proved that the identification of Mr. Beck by the female witnesses as the man who robbed them was a monstrous farce.

"I have proved that, so far from Mr. Beck being the 'double' of John Smith, he was utterly unlike him, except that each had a gray mustache. Beck had neither the noticeable scar at the point of the jaw nor the noticeable wart over one eye that are striking marks of identity in John Smith—marks which would not escape the most casual observer.

"I have proved that Beck's conviction in 1896 was secured by a device which was utterly unworthy of a British court of justice—a device so unfair and unjust that an innocent and inoffensive foreigner, a Norwegian who had sought the hospitality of our shores, was by its employment sent into penal servitude for seven years for the crimes of another man.

"I have proved that Mr. Beck was in 1904 convicted of repeating letter for letter, word for word, trick for trick, check for check, false address for false address, false name for false name, the frauds of 1877 and 1896, of which the authorities had absolute proof that he was innocent, and of which, though they had never remitted one day of his sentence, they had admitted that he was innocent.

"I have been careful to keep to the main issue, and have refrained from examining the side issues, some of which reveal most lamentable features in connection with our criminal procedure.

"I will prove one thing more, and leave the facts I have established to the judgment of the public.

"At the end of the report of the second trial of Adolf Beck, which took place at the Old Bailey on June 27, 1904 (Sessions Paper CXL., Part 837), are these words, printed as I give them below:

"'GUILTY. He then PLEADED GUILTY to a conviction of obtaining goods by false pretenses at this Court on February 26, 1896. Judgment respited.'

"Pleaded guilty to a former conviction! Adolf Beck pleaded guilty to nothing. How could he plead guilty, being an innocent man! He cried aloud when the charge of the first conviction was read aloud to him, 'As God is my witness, I was innocent then as I am innocent now.'

"The epilogue to the tragedy of our English Dreyfus is written in those damning words in the Sessions Paper, the official minutes of evidence in Central Criminal Court trials.

"Beck's last hope had perished. Once more a merciless fate had blinded the eyes and closed the ears of Justice to his innocence. He was to be immured in a convict cell for ten, perhaps for fourteen, years; he was to pass the closing years of his life a branded felon amid all the horrors of a convict prison. In all human probability he would die without ever seeing the light of freedom again, for he could not have borne this second torture. 161

"His voice, crying aloud for freedom, would be heard no more. Petitions for a reinvestigation of his case would be hopeless. He had been robbed of his last earthly chance of proving his innocence.

"Those words, 'The prisoner pleaded guilty to a former conviction,' would have damned him to the last day of his life.

"My painful task is ended.

"A foreigner, a stranger within our gates, a man of kindly heart and gentle ways, has been foully wronged. There is but one reparation we can make him. The people of this country owe him a testimonial of sympathy that shall endure and remain. On the site of his martyrdom there should rise a national monument. Let that monument take the form of a Court of Criminal Appeal. That is the one reparation that the English people can make to Adolf Beck for the foul wrong he has suffered in their midst."

In a sense the innocent man who is hanged may be regarded as better off than he who is called upon to endure lifelong imprisonment. There are plenty of examples of these judicial murders. Over a score of undoubted cases occurred in the first two decades of the last century, and since then there have been twice as many more. A notorious and awful case was that of Eliza Fenning, who, at eighteen years of age, was sent to the gallows upon the perjured evidence of an accomplice of the real murderer. The latter afterward confessed.

Another similar case occurred in 1850, when a man named Ross was executed for poisoning his young wife by mixing arsenic with her food. A few years later certain facts came to light, proving conclusively that the real criminal was a female acquaintance and confidante of the dead woman.

Thomas Perryman, again, was found guilty in 1879 of the murder of his aged mother on the very flimsiest of evidence. His sentence was commuted to penal servitude for life, and in the ordinary course of events he should now be free. More than 100,000 people have, at different times, petitioned for the release of this convict, and the highest judicial authorities have expressed their belief in his entire innocence of the crime imputed to him. Yet he has been compelled to drink his terrible cup to the bitter dregs.

In 1844 a gentleman named Barker was sentenced to penal servitude for life for a forgery of which he was afterward proved to have been wholly innocent. He served four years, and was then released and readmitted to practise as an attorney. In 1859, eleven years after having been "pardoned" he was, upon the recommendation of a Select Committee of the House of Commons, voted a sum of ,£5,000, "as a national acknowledgment of the wrong he had suffered from an erroneous prosecution."

The famous Edlingham case will doubtless be fresh in the minds of most people. In February, 1879, the village vicarage was entered by burglars, and a determined attempt was made to murder the aged incumbent. For this outrage two men, Brannagham and Murphy, were sentenced to lifelong imprisonment. After a lapse of nine years the crime was confessed to by two well-known criminals named Richardson and Edgell, the result being that the innocent convicts were released, with an honorarium of £800 apiece.

The eminent King's Counsel, Sir George Lewis, has openly said that he will not allow himself to speak of the way in which the "Edalji" trial was conducted, and he further adds: "I have it on undoubted authority that every M.P.' connected with the legal profession believes as I do that that man is innocent. And yet a declaration from such a source is allowed by the public to pass unnoticed. As I have before stated, it is not the business of the public, nor of individual citizens, to prove the innocence of any unhappy person whom the process of law selects for punishment; but it is the business of every citizen to see that the courts incontestably prove the guilt of any person accused of a crime before sentence is passed.' Neither condition was fulfilled in the case of the prisoner. I have studied the evidence, and say, from knowledge gained by fifteen years' association with criminals, that this unfortunate young man is innocent." Surely after the disclosures of the Adolf Beck case this one, on the word of Sir George Lewis, ought to receive unbiased consideration from the Home Office.

CHAPTER EIGHT

Religion in Prison Life

Dedication of New Chapel

ON our arrival at Aylesbury Prison there was no chapel. Divine service was held in one of the halls, in which the prisoners assembled each morning for twenty minutes of service. This arrangement had many disadvantages, and one of the ladies on the Board of Visitors came nobly to our relief with an offer to provide the prison with a chapel. The Home Office "graciously" accepted this generous proposition, and twelve months later it was completed and dedicated by the Lord Bishop of Reading. (It was burned to the ground since my departure from Aylesbury.)

On the day preceding the ceremony I was asked to assist in decorating the chapel with flowers kindly sent by Lady Rothschild. It was a delicate expression of sympathy for the prisoners, which she repeated on all high festival days. She was deeply affected when I told her how profoundly the women appreciated her recognition of a common humanity.

On the appointed day all work was suspended to enable the prisoners to be present. In the galleries were seated the families of the governor, chaplain, and doctor; at the right of the altar the generous donor of the chapel, Adeline, Duchess of Bedford, was seated with her friends. The organist played a prelude, and then the bishop, accompanied by the chaplain and the clergymen of the diocese, entered the chapel. After a hymn had been sung, a short service followed, and then the bishop stepped forward and, facing the altar, read the "dedication service." It was most impressive. Then followed a prayer and a hymn, and the service was over. The prisoners filed back to their respective cells and the visitors made the tour of the prison.

I was a patient in the infirmary at the time, but had received permission to attend the chapel. Before the Bishop of Reading left the prison he visited the sick, and as he passed my cell he stopped and spoke to me words of hope and encouragement, adding his blessing.

Influence of Religion upon Prisoners

Another occasion on which the Bishop of Reading visited the prison was the holding of a confirmation service. Many women of earnest minds in prison sought in this manner to prove the sincerity of their repentance and their resolution to live godly lives; and, with one exception, all those confirmed that day have remained true to their profession.

Penal servitude is a fiery test of one's religious convictions. One's faith is either strengthened and deepened or else it goes under altogether. I have witnessed many a sad spiritual shipwreck within those walls.

On a dark, gloomy day in October the rain pattered against the window of my cell and the wind howled dismally around that huge "house of sorrow." Now and then the sound of weeping broke upon the stillness, and I prayed in ray heart for the poor souls in travail whose pains had broken through the enforced rule of silence. There is no sound in all the world so utterly unnerving as the hopeless sob of the woman in physical isolation who may not be spiritually comforted. Separated from loved ones, beyond the reach of tender hands and voices, she has no one, as in former years, to share her sufferings or minister to her pain. Alone, one of a mass, with no one to care but the good God above; for "to suffer" thus is the punishment that man has decreed.

The humanizing influences, in my opinion, can be brought to bear upon prisoners with beneficial results only when supported by the advantages of religious teachings. During the early part of my sentence there were Scripture readers, laymen and laywomen, in all convict prisons, to assist the chaplain in his arduous duties; but, on the ground of expense, these have been dispensed with, thus practically removing the only means of administering the moral medicine which is essential to the cure of the habitual prisoner's mental disease.

A large amount of crime is due to physical and mental degeneration. Nevertheless, crime is also the result of lovelessness, when it is not a disease, and the true curative system should give birth to love in human souls. There is not a man or woman living so low but we can do something to better him or her, if we give love and sympathy in the service and have an all-embracing affection for both God and man.

If the future system is to treat the criminal in a curative or reformative way, rather than by punitive methods, the means to this end must certainly be increased. Even the worst woman can be approached through the emotional side of her nature. A kind word, a sympathetic look, a smile, a little commendation now and then, given by the officers in charge, would soon gain the respect and confidence of the prisoner, and thereby render her the more amenable to rules and regulations. A prisoner with whom I worked, and whose inner life by near association was revealed to me, had got into a very morbid, depressed state of mind. She was under close observation by the doctor's orders. Her penal record was not a good one; her hasty temper was continually getting her into trouble, and when she was punished she would brood over it.

Suicide of a Prisoner

One day she asked for permission to see me; the permission was refused. She made the request a second time, and, the fact coming to the knowledge of the chaplain, he advised that it be granted, believing, from his personal knowledge of my influence in the prison, that it would have a beneficial effect. I was allowed to see her, and after a few minutes' conversation she appeared brighter. I told her that the people of God have a promise of a Comforter from heaven to come to them and abide with them, even in tribulation and in prison. She promised me she would try to be more submissive and accept her punishment in a better spirit. For several days after she seemed to improve. But one afternoon she once more made the request to be allowed to see me. As none of the authorities were in the building at the time, and the chief matron could not take upon herself the responsibility of granting the request, it was refused. I felt rather anxious about it, but was helpless. At five o'clock that evening, just before supper was served, the woman was found dead in her cell; she had hanged herself to the window. She was only twenty-four years of age, and was serving a five years' sentence for shooting her betrayer under great provocation. The tragedy was naturally kept quiet; none of the prisoners knew of it until the following morning. How the truth got abroad I do not know, but when the doors were unlocked after breakfast, instead of the women passing out of their cells in the usual orderly way, they rushed out, shouting excitedly at the top of their voices: "M— has hanged herself;... she was driven to it!" In vain the officers tried to pacify them or to explain the true state of things; they would not listen, and continued to scream: "Don't talk to us—you are paid to say that! If you did not say that it was all right you would be turned out of the gates!" And the uproar increased. As I have already stated, the "Star Class" was sandwiched between two wards of habitual criminals, and we had the benefit of every disturbance. During the excitement one of the ringleaders caught sight of me and shouted: "Mrs. Maybrick, is it true that M— was driven to it?"

The tumult was increasing and was growing beyond the control of the warder, when the chief matron, becoming alarmed, sent up word that I might explain to the women. Accompanied by an officer, I did so, and in a few minutes the uproar calmed down and the women returned quietly to their cells. I have reason to believe that I always had the full confidence of my fellow prisoners; they were quick to know and appreciate that I had their welfare at heart, and that I never countenanced any disobedience or breach of the rules. A first offender, under sentence for many years, will suffer from the punishment according as she maintains or damages her self-respect.

Tragedies in Prison

Above others there are four tragic prison episodes which, once witnessed, can never be forgotten:

1. Breaking bad news to a prisoner—telling her that a dear one in the outside world is dying, and that she may not go to him; that she must wait in terrible suspense until the last message is sent, no communication in the meantime being permitted.

2. Receiving an intimation of the death of a beloved father, mother, brother or sister, husband or child, whose visits and letters have been the sole comfort and support of that prisoner's hard lot.

3. The loss of reason by a prisoner who was not strong enough to endure the punishment decreed by Act of Parliament.

4. The suicide, who prefers to trust to the mercy of God rather than suffer at the hands of man.

Why should a woman be considered less loving, less capable of suffering, because she is branded with the name of "convict?" She may be informed that her nearest and dearest are dying, but the rules will permit no departure to relieve the heart-breaking suspense. In the world at large telegrams may be sent and daily bulletins received, but not in the convict's world.

Death is a solemn event under any circumstances, and reverence for the dead is inculcated by our religion, but to die in prison is a thing that every inmate dreads with inexpressible horror. When a prisoner is at the point of death, she is put into a cell alone, or into a ward, if there is one vacant. There she lies alone. The nurse and infirmary officers come and go; her fellow prisoners gladly minister to her; the doctor and chaplain are assiduous in their attentions; but she is nevertheless alone, cut off from her kin, tended by the servants of the law instead of the servants of love, and it is only at the very last that her loved ones may come and say their farewell. Oh! the pathos, the anguish of such partings—who shall describe them? And when all is over, and the law has no longer any power over the body it has tortured, it may be claimed and taken away.

The case of the prisoner who becomes 177 insane is no less harrowing. She is kept in the infirmary with the other patients for three months. If she does not recover her reason within that period, she is certified by three doctors as insane and then removed to the criminal lunatic asylum. In the meantime the peace and rest of the other sick persons in the infirmary are disturbed by her ravings, and their feelings wrought upon by the daily sight of a demented fellow creature.

And the suicide! To see the ghastly and distorted features of a fellow prisoner, with whom one has worked and suffered, killed by her own hands—such scenes as these haunted me for weeks; and it needed all my reliance on God to throw off the depression that inevitably followed.

Moral Effect of Harsh Prison Regime

Have you ever tried to realize what kind of life that must be in which the sight of a child's face and the sound of a child's voice are ever absent; in which there are none of the sweet influences of the home; the daily intercourse with those we love; the many trifling little happenings, so unimportant in themselves, but which go so far to make up the sum of human happiness? It commences with the clangor of bells and the jingling of keys, and closes with the banging of hundreds of doors, while the after silence is broken only by shrieks and blasphemies, the trampling of many feet, and the orders of warders.

In the winter the prisoners get up in the dark, and breakfast in the dark, to save the expense of gas. The sense of touch becomes very acute, as so much has to be done without light. Until I had served three years of my sentence I had not been allowed to see my own face. Then a looking-glass, three inches long, was placed in my cell. I have often wondered how this deprivation could be harmonized with a purpose to enforce tidiness or cleanliness in a prisoner. The obvious object in depriving prisoners of the only means through which they can reasonably be expected to conform to the official standard of facial cleanliness is to eradicate woman's assumed innate sense of vanity; but whether or no it succeeds in this, certain it is that cleanliness becomes a result of compulsion rather than of a natural womanly impulse. Also she must maintain the cleanliness of her prison cell on an ounce of soap per week. After I left Aylesbury I heard that the steward had received orders from the Home Office to reduce this enormous quantity. If true it will leave the unfortunate prisoners with three-quarters of an ounce of soap weekly wherewith to maintain that cleanliness which is said to be next to godliness. The prisoners are allowed a hot bath once a week, but in the interval they may not have a drop of hot water, except by the doctor's orders.

Attacks of Levity

All human instincts cannot be crushed, even by an act of Parliament, and sometimes the prisoners indulge in a flight of levity, which is, however, promptly stopped by the officer in charge. But even wilfulness and levity are to some a relief from the perpetual silence. A young girl, fifteen years of age, came in on a conviction of penal servitude for life. In a fit of passion she had strangled a child of which she had charge. In consideration of her youth and the medical evidence adduced at her trial, sentence of death was commuted. She was in the "Star Class," and it aroused my indignation to witness her sufferings. A mature woman may submit to the inevitable patiently, as an act of faith or as a proof of her philosophy; but a child of that age has neither faith nor philosophy sufficient to support her against this repressive system of torture. At times, however, the girl had attacks of levity which manifested themselves in most amusing ways. One day she was put out to work in the officers' quarters and told to black-lead a grate. With a serious face she set to work. Presently the officer asked whether she had finished her task, to which she meekly replied "Yes," at the same time lifting her face, which, to the utter amazement of the female warder, had been transformed from a white to a brightly polished black one.

On another occasion she was told that she would be wanted in the infirmary. She was suffering great pain at the time, and had begged the doctor to extract a tooth. When the infirmary nurse unlocked her door she was found in bed. This is strictly against the rules, unless the prisoner has special permission from the doctor to lie down during the day. Of course, the officer ordered her to get up at once, to which she replied, "I can't." "Why not?" asked the officer. "Because I can't," the girl repeated. Whereupon the officer lifted off the bed covering to see what was amiss. To her astonishment she saw that the child had got inside the mattress (which I described in the beginning as a long sack stuffed with the fiber of the coconut), and had drawn the end of it on a string around her neck, so that nothing but her head was visible.

It has been said that no apples are so sweet as those that are stolen, and the great pleasure the women in prison derive from their surreptitious levity is because it can so rarely be indulged in, and the opportunities for its expression must always be stolen.

There is an axiom in prison, "The worse the woman, the better the prisoner." As one goes about the prison, and observes those women who are permitted little privileged tasks, such as tidying the garden, cleaning the chapel, or any of the light and semi-responsible tasks which convicts like, one will notice the privileged are not, as a rule, the young or respectably brought up, but old, professional criminals. They know the rules of the prison, they spend the greater part of their lives there, and they know exactly how to behave so as to earn the maximum of marks; their object is to get out in the shortest possible time, and to have as light work as possible while they are in. The officers like them because they know their work without having to be taught. "There is no servant like an old thief," I have heard it said. "They do good work." This is quite typical of a certain kind of prisoner who is the mainstay of the prisons.

The conviction of young girls to penal servitude is shocking, for it destroys the chief power of prevention that prisons are supposed to possess, and accustoms the young criminal to a reality which has far less terror for her than the idea of it had. Prison life is entirely demoralizing to any girl under twenty years of age, and it is to prevent such demoralizing influence upon young girls that some more humane system of punishment should be enacted,

Self-Discipline

In saying a word on what is, perhaps, best described as "prison self-discipline," I trust the reader will acquit me of any motive other than a desire that it may result in some sister in misfortune deriving benefit from a similar course. That the state of mind in which one enters upon the life of a convict has some influence on conduct—whether she does so with a consciousness of innocence or otherwise—should, perhaps, go without saying. Nevertheless, innocent or guilty, a proper self-respect cannot fail to be helpful, be the circumstances what they may; and from the moment I crossed Woking's grim threshold until the last day when I passed from the shadow and the gloom of Aylesbury into God's free sunlight, I adhered strictly to a determination that I would come out of the ordeal—if ever—precisely as I had entered upon it; that no loving eyes of mother or friends should detect in my habits, manners, or modes of thought or expression the slightest deterioration.

Accordingly I set about from the very start to busy myself—and this was no small helpfulness in filling the dreary hours of the seemingly endless days of solitary confinement—keeping my cell in order and ever making the most of such scant material for adornment as the rules permitted. Little enough in this way, it may be imagined, falls to a convict's lot. Indeed, the sad admission is forced that nearly every semblance of refinement is maintained at one's peril, for "motives" receive small consideration in the interpretation of prison rules, however portentously they may have loomed in the process that placed an innocent woman under the shadow of the scaffold, and only by grace of a commutation turned her into a "life" convict.

Come what would, I was determined not to lose my hold on the amenities of my former social position, and, though I had only a wooden stool and table, they were always spotless, my floor was ever brightly polished, while my tin pannikins went far to foster the delusion that I was in possession of a service of silver.

Confinement in a cell is naturally productive of slothful habits and indifference to personal appearance. I felt it would be a humiliation to have it assumed that I could or would deteriorate because of my environment. I therefore made it a point never to yield to that feeling of indifference which is the almost universal outcome of prison life. I soon found that this self imposed regimen acted as a wholesome moral tonic, and so, instead of falling under the naturally baneful influences of my surroundings, I strove, with ever-renewed spiritual strength, to rise above them. At first the difference that marked me from so many of my fellow prisoners aroused in them something like a feeling of resentment; but when they came to know me this soon wore off, and I have reason to believe that my example of unvarying neatness and civility did not fail in influencing others to look a bit more after their personal appearance and to modify their speech. At any rate, it had this effect: Aylesbury Prison is the training-school for female warders for all county prisons. Having served a month's probation here, they are recommended, if efficient in enforcing the prison "discipline," for transference to analogous establishments in the counties. It happened not infrequently, therefore, that new-comers were taken to my cell as the model on which all others should be patterned.

I partook of my meals, coarse and unappetizing as the food might be, after the manner I had been wont in the diningroom of my own home; and, though unseen, I never permitted myself to use my fingers (as most prisoners invariably did) where a knife, fork, or spoon would be demanded by good manners. Neither did I permit myself, either at table (though alone) or elsewhere, to fall into slouchy attitudes, even when, because of sickness, it was nearly impossible for me to hold up my head.

I speak of this because of the almost universal tendency among prisoners to mere animality. "What matters it?" is the general retort. Accordingly, the average convict keeps herself no cleaner than the discipline strenuously exacts, while all their attitudes express hopeless indifference, callous carelessness, to a degree that often lowers them to the behavior of the brutes of the field. The repressive system can neither reform nor raise the nature or habits of prisoners.

Need of Women Doctors and Inspectors

Women doctors and inspectors should be appointed in all female prisons. Otherwise what can be expected of a woman of small mental resources, shut in on herself, often unable to read or write with any readiness; of bad habits; with a craving for low excitement; whose chief pleasure has been in the grosser kind of animal delight? The mind turns morbidly inward; the nerves are shattered. Although the dark cell is no longer used, mental light is still excluded. Recidivation is more frequent with women than with men. The jail taint seems to sink deeper into woman's nature, and at Aylesbury numbers of the more abandoned ones are seldom for long out of the male warders' hands.

Chastening Effect of Imprisonment on the Spirit

For a considerable period I was given work in the officers' mess. Their quarters are in a detached building within the prison precincts, and are reached by crossing a small grass-plot which separates it from the prison. Each officer has a small bedroom, in which she sleeps and passes her time when off duty. All meals are served in the mess-room, and consist of breakfast at seven o'clock, lunch on turn between nine and eleven, dinner at twelve-thirty, tea at five, and supper whenever they are off duty. The cooking is excellent and varied. A matron is in charge of the commissariat department, and has four prisoners of the "Star Class" working under her. I did scullery work, which consisted of washing up all the crockery, glass, knives, forks, and spoons used at these five meals, besides all the pots and pans required in their preparation. As a staff of twenty-five sat down to these frequent meals daily, the work was very hard and quite beyond my strength. The "Star Class" of workers should not be kept at it more than six months at a time. Some of the life women have been in the kitchen and mess-room as long as three and four years, and, as neither the culinary arrangements nor the ventilation are modem, the consequent physical and mental depression arising from these defects, and the monotony of the work, is only too apparent.

I was not feeling well at the time, and soon after I had a long illness—a nervous breakdown, due partly to insomnia and partly to the unrelieved strain and stress of years of hard labor. My recovery was very slow. I was in the infirmary about eighteen months, and was glad when finally discharged, as the intervals between my letters and visits were shorter when I was in discipline quarters and could earn more marks. During the long years of my imprisonment I learned many lessons I needed, perhaps, to have learned during my earlier life; but, thank God, I was no criminal! I was being punished for that of which I was innocent. I believe it is God's task to judge and ours to endure, but I could not understand what his plans and his purposes were. I believed they were good, although I could not see how eternity itself could make up for my sufferings. Perhaps they were intended to work out some good to others, by ways I should never know, until I saw with the clear eyes of another world. Still, the external conditions of life acted on my body and mind, and I scarcely knew at times how to bear them. I could not have endured them without God's sustaining-grace. I used often to repeat these lines:

>"With patience, then, the course of duty run;
>God never does nor suffers to be done
>But that which you would do if you could see
>The end of all events as well as he."

A Death-bed Incident

A woman lay dying in a near-by cell. Of the sixty years of her life she had spent forty within prison walls. What that life had been I will not say, but when she was in the agony of death she called to me: "I don't know anything about your God, but if he has made you tender and loving to a bad lot like me, I know he will not be hard on a poor soul who never had a chance. Give me a kiss, dear lass, before I go. No one has kissed me since my mother died."

CHAPTER NINE

My Last Years in Prison

I am Set to Work in the Library

WHEN I recovered from my nervous was given lighter employment, and went into the library. I was now the only prisoner in the building who had suffered under the hardships of the old system at Woking Prison, all the rest of those who came with me having in the interim returned to the world. In fact, I was the only one who had served over ten years.

My task in the library was to assist the school mistress and to change the library books twice a week. They were carried from cell to cell, and this represented the handling of over two hundred and fifty books. In addition to this, I had to be breakdown, "literary nurse," whose duties were to attend to worn-out books, binding up their wounds and prolonging their days of usefulness; doing cataloguing and entry work; to print the name of each prisoner on a card placed over her cell door; to copy hymns, and to make scrapbooks for the illiterate prisoners, besides other miscellaneous duties.

The library was a very good one and contained not only the latest novels, but philosophical works and books for study; also a limited number in French and German. To these were added religious works, especially poetry, and sermons for Sunday reading. I found a choice collection to help me support the Sabbath day, for the suspended animation makes a day of misery of the "day of rest." One could not read all day without tiring, and the absence of week-day work usually made it a day of heavy, creeping depression. There are two periods of exercise, and chapel morning and afternoon. The remainder of the time the prisoners are locked in their cells. Reading was my only solace; from first to last I read every moment that I could call my own. The best index of the quality of the books was that every volume was read or examined by the chaplain and his staff before it was admitted to the library. If it contained any articles on prison life or matters relating to prisoners, these were always carefully cut out.

From my observations I consider that prison schoolmasters and schoolmistresses are overburdened with miscellaneous and incompatible duties. No one needs to be told that the average prisoner is a slow learner, and that even a dull boy or girl is a better pupil than a grown man or woman plodding along in the first steps of knowledge, and who is taught, not in a class, but in a cell. Yet the schoolmaster or schoolmistress has to devote hours daily to teaching, to help in letter-writing, in the office work, in the distribution of library books, in the library work; and now that their number is likewise reduced on the ground of expense, the pressure of their work is out of all proportion to the hours within which it can be reasonably performed.

I have always been fond of reading, and during my leisure hours I got through a large number of books. This was between noon and half-past one, and seven and eight in the evening, when my light had to be put out.

Newspapers Forbidden

The rules forbid that any public news be conveyed to the prisoners, either at visits or by letters. This seems to be a very short-sighted view to take of the matter. To allow newspapers in the prison might, of course, lead to cipher communications to prisoners from their friends; but no harm can possibly come of allowing information regarding public affairs of national interest to be conveyed through the legitimate channels of letters and visits. It would give the prisoners fresh food for thought, and tend greatly to relieve that vacuity of mind which is the outcome of lack of knowledge of external things, and of the monotony of their lives; it would also make a pause in their broodings over their cases, which is the sole subject of their thoughts and conversations when permitted to converse at all.

How Prisoners Learn of Great Events

The lowering of the prison flag told us of the death of Queen Victoria [January 22, 1901], although we had heard several days before that she was sinking. When King Edward was dangerously ill it was talked of among the officers, and the prisoners, through me, asked that special prayers might be said in the chapel.

When Mafeking was relieved and when peace with the Boers was declared, flags were hoisted. Jubilee and Coronation days were the only occasions I remember when we had any relaxation of prison rules, and then there was much disappointment, since in lieu of a mitigation of our sentences, as was the case in India, they gave us extra meat and plum pudding.

Strict Discipline of Prison Officers

I have served under three governors, each of whom was an intelligent and conspicuously humane man. They knew their prisoners and tried to understand them, but there is not much a governor can do for them of his own initiative. I consider that he who holds this responsible position should have more of a free hand, and be allowed to use his discretion in all ordinary matters pertaining to the prison discipline and welfare of the prisoners.

They were all advanced disciplinarians. The routine reeled itself off with mechanical precision. The rules were enforced and carried out to the letter. The deadly monotony never varied; all days are alike; r weeks, months, years slowly accumulate, and, in the meantime, the mental rust is eating into the weary brain, and the outspoken cry rises up daily—"How long, O Lord! how long?"

The officers are almost as keen as the governor in their efforts to keep things up to the mark. It is seldom they allow prisoners under their observation or supervision any slight relaxation which nature may demand, but the rules forbid. They dislike to punish a woman, and in their hearts make many excuses for the black sheep.

Their High Character

As a class, with few exceptions, the prison staff is worthy of respect and confidence, and might be trusted with any task. The patience, civility, and self-control which the officers exhibit under the most trying circumstances, as a rule, mark them as men and women possessing a high sense of duty, not only as civil servants, but as Christians.

Nervous Strain of Their Duties

The hours of work are long, the nervous strain is incessant. I could wish that those in high places showed a little more appreciation of what these faithful servants do, and were not so sparing of their praise and commendation. The small remuneration they receive cannot make up for the deprivation of the amenities of life which the prison service entails. Two writers on prison life have expressed themselves in widely different ways regarding the warders and officers. One writer compares them to slave and cattle-drivers; another expresses surprise that they are as good as they are. As, I trust, an impartial observer, I agree with the latter opinion. Experience has taught me that, in most cases, if the prisoner is amiable and willing, the officer on her part is ready to meet the prisoner fully half way—at all events, as far as circumstances and duty will permit, for the continual daily changes of duty, from ward to ward and hall to hall, make it nearly impossible for any officer to acquire a true knowledge of the character of those under her charge.

It would be interesting if a trained psychologist could watch and report upon the insidious effect of the repressive rules and regulations of a prison on the more impressionable officers and prisoners. When such officers first enter this service they are natural women with a natural demeanor and expression of countenance. After a time, however, the molding effects of "standing orders" become apparent in the sternness of their expression, the harsh tones of their voices, and the abruptness of their manner.

Standing Orders for Warders

These "standing orders" may be paraphrased as follows:

"You must not do this or say that, or look sympathetic or friendly, or converse with prisoners in any way. You must always suspect them of wishing to do something underhand, sly, and contrary to orders. You must never let them for a moment out of your sight, or permit them to suppose that you have either trust or confidence in them. It is your duty to see that the means of punishment devised by the Penal Code are faithfully carried out. You are not to trouble yourself about the result upon the prisoner—that is the affair of the Government."

Any familiarity on the part of an officer with a prisoner is strictly forbidden by the rules of prison service, and the slightest manifestation of the sort would entail serious punishment on the officer. Surely this is not as it should be; on the contrary, greater discretionary power should be permitted to officers in their relations with prisoners, for the influence for good which a kind, well-disposed officer could exert upon a prisoner is incalculable. But all this possible influence for good is denied expression by the spirit of mistrust and suspicion which pervades the entire prison administration. This is one of the most regrettable features of the system. No officer is trusted by her superior, and no prisoner, however exemplary her conduct, may be trusted by any one officially connected with the institution.

An officer who commits a breach of any rule laid down for her may be fined a sum varying from one to ten shillings, and if the offense is a grave one she may be discharged.

Crime a Mental Disease

When will those connected with prisons awake to the fact that the criminal is mentally diseased? Ninety-nine out of a hundred criminals, when not such by accident, through poverty, or environment, come to their lot through inherited, malformed brains. It ought to be the sacred duty of earnest men to deal kindly, intelligently, and patiently with them. The prison, which is now a dreadful place of punishment and humiliation, ought to be made a home of regeneration and reformation, in which intelligent effort is made to raise the prisoner to a higher level; and this surely is not done by withdrawing all the refining influences.

I hope the time is not far off when men and women will take more of a heart interest in prisoners, and when, no matter how low they may have sunk, an opportunity to live honestly will be given them on their release; when the society against which they have sinned will treat them so kindly that for very shame they will seek to do better, and repentance shall enter into the most darkened soul. The "eye for an eye and tooth for a tooth" doctrine is not a part of the Christian dispensation. Our Lord Jesus Christ gave his last supreme lesson, as he turned toward the thief at his side on the cross, and there put an end to that old law forever.

Something Good in the Worst Criminal

There is some good to be found in the worst criminal, which, if nourished by patience and sympathy, will grow into more good. I speak from a large, intimate personal experience, for during my imprisonment it was my happy fortune to evoke kindly reciprocations from some of the worst and most degraded characters. I will cite an instance.

One day I was crossing the hall when a fight occurred. I cannot describe it—it was too horrible. The crowd surged toward me, and I was being drawn in among the combatants, when one of them, catching sight of me, stepped out with a face streaming with blood, and pushed me into an open cell, closing the door after me. When I thanked her the next day she replied:

"Why, bless your heart, Mrs. Maybrick, did you think I would let them hurt a hair of your head?"

I believe I had the sympathy and respect of all my fellow prisoners, and when I left Aylesbury, my feelings were those of mingled relief and regret. I could not but feel attached to those with whom I had lived and suffered and worked for so many weary years. I knew, perhaps, more of the life history of these poor women, their inner thoughts and feelings, than any one else in the prison. In suffering, in sympathy, in pity, we were all akin. In the association hour they would bring me their letters from home to read, and show me the photographs of their children or other dear ones, while tears would course down their cheeks at the memory of happier days.

Need of Further Prison Reform

Many opinions have been written regarding prisons, but with few exceptions they are the observations of outsiders, which means, they must of necessity be to a certain extent superficial.

I have touched only a few spots of the great diseased system of prison management, but what public opinion did to ameliorate past abuses, public opinion can still do to improve the treatment of to-day's criminal. A little over a hundred years ago there were thirty-four offenses in England punishable by capital punishment. To-day there is only one. Charles Dickens did more than any agency toward doing away with imprisonment for debt, yet last year there were no less than eleven thousand prisoners in confinement for debt in English prisons. How many of these have since joined the ranks of the criminals through loss of self-respect? What has been the effect upon their wives and families? Why is a man imprisoned for debt? Certainly not to enable him to pay it. He can earn nothing while in prison, where he is supported at the expense of the state; and if he has a wife or family, they either become dependent on the rates, or incur debts which he will have to pay on his release. Again, he may not improbably lose his employment, and have to look out for another when liberated, and his imprisonment does not make it more easy, either to procure work or to perform it efficiently. The ground of imprisonment is dishonesty. But is not actual dishonesty sufficiently met by the criminal law? In what sense is the debtor dishonest? Is it meant that he has money in his pocket and refuses to pay his debts? Is it not rather that he ought to have had money? It is proved perhaps that he is earning so much per week, possibly, but how long had he been earning and how long was he out of employment before that? Has he had sickness? There have been many instances where a man was in the hospital when the committal order was made, and was seized and carried off to prison immediately on discharge. If non-payment of a debt is not a crime, why is he in prison for it? If it is a crime, why has he not the benefit of a trial by jury on the ability or inability of paying his debts? And why should not the Home Office or other appellate tribunal have the power of revising his sentence? If the debtor has goods that can be seized, let them be seized; if there is money coming to him, let the creditor attach it; if it comes within the scope of the bankruptcy law, let him be adjudicated and examined on oath to every shilling that he has received or spent. But why, in the name of justice and humanity, treat him as a criminal, prevent him from earning his bread, and make him an incumbrance on the State, exposing his wife and daughter to ruin, degrading him, lowering his self-respect, and subjecting him to the taint of the prison atmosphere, without satisfactory evidence of his ability to pay at the time of committal? Several prisoners that I came in contact with were made criminals because their husbands had left their families destitute because imprisoned for debt.

CHAPTER TEN

My Release

I Learn the Time When My Sentence Will Terminate

AFTER I had been incarcerated for a few years I found out that it was usual in the case of a life convict who has earned good marks to have her sentence brought up for consideration after she has served fifteen years. A life sentence usually means twenty years, and three months is taken off each year as a reward for good conduct. In February, 1903, I was definitely informed that my case would follow the ordinary course. I have been accused of obtaining my release by "trickery," but these facts speak for themselves.

The impression has also been given by the press that great leniency was shown in my case, and that through the intervention of friends the Home Office released me before the expiration of my sentence. No exceptional leniency whatever was shown in my case. It depends upon the prisoner herself whether she is released at an earlier period or serves the full term of her sentence. By an unbroken record of good conduct I reduced my life sentence, which is twenty years, to fifteen years; this expired on the 25th of July, 1904.

The Dawn of Liberty

As a giant refreshed by sleep, the prison awakens to life, and the voices of officers, the clang of doors, the ringing of bells echo throughout the halls. What does it portend? Is it the arrival of some distinguished visitor from the Home Office? Then I hear the sound of approaching footsteps, as they come nearer and nearer and then stop at my cell door. The governor ushers in three gentlemen—one tall and dark and handsome, but with a stern face; another short, with a white beard and blue eyes which looked at me somewhat coldly; of the third I have no distinct recollection. The tall gentleman conversed pleasantly for several minutes about my work and myself, then passed out on his tour of inspection. I did not know at the time who these visitors were, but learned later that the gentleman who spoke to me was the Secretary of State, Sir Matthew White-Ridley;

one of his companions was Sir Kenelm Digby, and the other Sir Evelyn Ruggles-Brise, the chairman of the Prison Committee, who takes a really humane interest in the welfare of the convicts.

One morning, a week later, I was summoned to appear before the governor. It is an ordeal to be dreaded by any one who has broken the rules, but I knew I had not, and therefore concluded that I was wanted in connection with my work. When I entered the office he looked up with a kindly smile, which was also reflected in the face of the chief matron. My attention was arrested. I stood silently waiting for him to speak. After searching among some papers on the table, he picked up one and read something to the following effect: "The prisoner, P 29, Florence E. Maybrick, is to be informed that the Secretary of State has decided to grant her discharge from prison when she has completed fifteen years of her sentence, conditional upon her conduct."

For a moment I failed to grasp the full meaning of these words, but when I did—how shall I describe the mingled feelings of joy and thankfulness, of relief and hope, with which I was overwhelmed! I returned to my cell dazed by the unexpected message for which for so many long, weary years I had hoped and prayed.

How anxiously I waited for those last few months to pass!

The Release

It was Christmas Eve of 1903. I had helped to decorate the chapel with evergreens, which is the only way in which the greatest festival of the church's year is kept in prison. There is no rejoicing allowed prisoners; no festival meal of roast beef and plum pudding, only the usual prison diet; and the sad memories of happier days are emphasized by our bare cells with their maximum of cleanliness and minimum of comfort. But to me it was the last Christmas in that "house of sorrow," and my heart felt the dawning of a brighter day. Only four weeks more and I would have passed out of its grim gates forever! How I counted those days, and yet how I shrank from going once more into the world that had been so cruel, so hostile, so unmerciful, in spite of the fact that there was no proof that I was the guilty woman they assumed me to be! But kind friends and loving hearts were waiting to greet me, to give me refuge and comfort.

On Saturday, the 23d of January, my mother visited me at Aylesbury Prison for the last time. How many weary and sad hours we had passed in that visiting-room! Our hearts were too full for much conversation, and it was with broken voices that we discussed the arrangements made for my departure on the following Monday.

The last Sunday I spent in prison I felt like one in a dream. I could not realize that to morrow, the glad to-morrow, would bring with it freedom and life. In the evening I was sent for to say "Good-by" to the governor. Besides the chief matron and the one who was to be my escort to Truro, no one was aware of the day or hour of my departure from Aylesbury. Not a word had been said to the other prisoners. I should like to have said farewell to them, also to the officers whom I had known for fourteen years (for several had come with us from Woking Prison); but I thought it best to pass into my new life as quietly as possible. At my earnest request the Home Office consented to allow my place of destination to be kept a secret. I felt that I should derive more benefit from the change of my new environment and association with others, if my identity and place of retreat were not known to the public.

On Monday, the 25th of January, I was awakened early, and after laying aside, for the last time, the garments of shame and disgrace, I was clothed once more in those that represent civilization and respectability. I descended to the court below, and, accompanied by the chief matron and my escort, passed silently through the great gates and out of the prison. At half-past six a cab drove quietly up, and the matron and I silently stepped in and were driven away to the Aylesbury Station. On our arrival in London we proceeded at once to Paddington Station. The noise and the crowds of people everywhere bewildered me.

In Retreat at Truro

After an uneventful journey we arrived at Truro at six p.m., and drove at once to the Home of the Community of the Epiphany, where I stayed during the remainder of my term of six months. I am told that some comment has been made on the fact that the Home was a religious retreat, and that I ought to have been sent to a secular one instead. I went there entirely of my own desire. On our arrival there I bade a last farewell to my kind companion—one of the sweetest women it has been my privilege to meet. The Mother Superior, who had visited me three months previously at Aylesbury Prison, received me tenderly, and at once conducted me to my room. How pure and chaste everything looked after the cold, bare walls of my prison cell! How the restful quiet soothed my jarred and weakened nerves, and, above all, what comforting balm the dear Mother Superior and the sweet sisters poured into the wounds of my riven soul!

I look back upon the six months spent within those sacred walls as the most peaceful and the happiest—in the true sense—of my life. The life there is so calm, so holy, and yet so cheerful, that one becomes infected, so that the sad thoughts flee away, the drooping hands are once more uplifted, and the heart strengthened to perform the work that a loving God may have ordained.

I passed several hours of each day working in the sewing-room with the sisters. During my leisure time I read much, and when the weather was fine delighted in taking long walks within the lovely grounds that surround the Home. I did not go out in the country, nor attend the services on Sunday at the Cathedral.

I left Truro on the 20th of July a free woman—with a ticket-of-leave, it is true, but as I am exempt from police supervision even in England, I have no need to consider it in America or elsewhere.

By the courtesy of the American Ambassador, the Hon. Joseph H. Choate, I was provided with an escort to accompany me and my companion on our journey from Truro to Rouen, France.

The Hon. John Hay,[*] Secretary of State, Washington; the Hon. Joseph H. Choate, Mr. Henry White, Charge d'Affaires, and Mr. Carter, Secretary of Embassy, at London, have always been most earnest in my cause. I deeply appreciate their untiring efforts in my behalf.

*As a young man, John Hay had been a secretary in the White House to Lincoln.—Ed. 2015

I Come to America

After staying with my mother for three weeks, on the advice of my counselors, Messrs. Hayden & Yarrell, of Washington, District of Columbia, I decided to return to America with Mr. Samuel V. Hayden and his charming wife. I longed to be once more with my own people, and it was only physical weakness and nervous prostration that prevented me from doing so immediately upon my release. I met these good friends at Antwerp, Belgium, and sailed from there on the Red Star Line steamship Vaderland for New York. My name was entered on the passenger list as Rose Ingraham, that I might secure more quiet and privacy; but when we were a few days out the fact of my identity became known, and with few exceptions the greatest courtesy, consideration, and delicacy were shown in the demeanor of the passengers toward me. If any of these should read these lines I would herewith express to them my grateful thanks and appreciation; while toward the captain and officers of the Vaderland I feel especially indebted for their unwearied courtesy and consideration.

When I first caught sight of the Statue of Liberty, I, perhaps more than any one on board, realized the full meaning of what it typifies, and I felt my heart stirred to its depths at the memory of what all my countrymen and countrywomen had done for me during the dark days of my past, to prove that they still carried me in their hearts, though the great ocean rolled between, and that I had not been robbed of the high privilege of being an American citizen.

We arrived at New York on the 23d of August. It was a "red-letter" day. Once more, after many years of suffering and when I had long despaired of ever seeing the beloved faces of my friends again, my feet once again pressed the sacred soil of my native land.

A time will come when the world will acknowledge that the verdict which was passed upon me is absolutely untenable. But what then? Who shall give back the years I have spent within prison walls; the friends by whom I am forgotten; the children to whom I am dead;

the sunshine; the winds of heaven; my woman's life, and all I have lost by this terrible injustice?

The innocents—my children—one a baby of three years, the other a boy of seven, I had left behind in the world. They had been taught to believe that their mother was guilty, and, like their father, was to them dead. They have grown up to years of understanding under another name. I know nothing about them. When the pathos of all this touches the reader's heart he will realize the tragedy of my case.

During the early years of my imprisonment I received my children's photographs once a year; also several friendly letters from Mr. Thomas Maybrick, with information about them. But as time passed on, these ceased altogether. When I could endure the silence no longer I instructed Mr. R. S. Cleaver, of Liverpool—who had been the solicitor in my case, and to whose unwavering faith and kindness I owe a debt I can never hope to repay—to write to Mr. Michael Maybrick to forward fresh photographs of my boy and girl. To this request Mr. Thomas Maybrick replied that Mr. Michael Maybrick refused to permit it. When the matter was further urged Mr. Michael Maybrick himself wrote to the governor to inform me that my son, who had been made acquainted with the history of the case, did not wish either his own or his sister's photograph to be sent to me.

Time may heal the deepest wounds when the balm of love and sympathy is poured into them. It is well; for if mental wounds proved as fatal as those of the body, the prison death-roll would indeed be a long one.

PART TWO-ANALYSIS OF THE MAYBRICK CASE

Introduction

THE jury's verdict of guilty was rendered on August 7, 1889. The evidence at the trial, as well as the learned judge's "summing up," was reported almost verbatim in the English press. The result was that, not only in Liverpool, but in almost every city, town, and village of the United Kingdom, men and women of every class and grade of society arrived at the conclusion that the verdict was erroneous—as not founded upon evidence, but upon the biased and misleading summing up of the case by the mentally incompetent judge. Within a few days my lawyers, the Messrs. Cleaver, of Liverpool, who had notified the press that they would supply forms of petition, were inundated with applications. For the first two days they issued one thousand a day, and I have been informed that no less than five thousand petitions for a reprieve, representing nearly half a million signatures, were sent to the Home Secretary within the following ten days. In response to these, the Home Office issued to the press the following decision:

"After the fullest consideration, and after taking the best medical and legal advice that could be obtained, the Home Secretary advised Her Majesty to respite the capital punishment of Florence Elizabeth Maybrick and to commute the punishment to penal servitude for life; inasmuch as, although the evidence leads to the conclusion that the prisoner administered and attempted to administer arsenic to her husband with intent to murder him, yet it does not wholly exclude a reasonable doubt whether his death was in fact caused by the administration of arsenic."

Illogical Position of Home Secretary

Thus it will be seen that the Home Secretary, Mr. Matthews, ignored the important statement of the judge at the trial, when, in giving emphasis to his remarks, he told the jury that: "It is essential to this charge that the man died of arsenic. This question must be the foundation of a judgment unfavorable to the prisoner, that he died of arsenic." Then Mr. Matthews, on reviewing the evidence given at the trial, finding it impossible to justify the verdict, because the evidence "does not wholly exclude a reasonable doubt whether his [James Maybrick's] death was in fact caused by the administration of arsenic," which question was to be the foundation of a judgment unfavorable to me, instead of giving his prisoner the benefit of the reasonable doubt, took it upon himself to apply the spirit of the law and of the constitution, by making use of a wrongful conviction for one offense charged in order to punish me for a different offense for which I had never been tried, but with which he, without any public trial, charged me, viz., "administering and attempting to administer arsenic" to my husband.

New Evidence of Innocence Ignored

These charges, made by Mr. Matthews in 1889, have never been defined; nor has any statement been submitted to me or my legal advisers of the evidence relied on to prove them; nor have I been afforded an opportunity of being heard by counsel in answer to them, nor of pleading anything in reply to them. Had a second trial been granted me, I should have seen the evidence upon which the new charges were made against me, and in open court I could have confronted the witnesses. But Mr. Matthews sentenced me to penal servitude for life (without giving me a chance to defend myself against the charges) which involved nine months' solitary confinement in my case—in itself a most excessive punishment for the untried and, consequently, unproven charges. He sent me to suffer fourteen and one-half years on suspicion—a suspicion not warranted by any evidence given at the trial. The new evidence, which has been obtained since my conviction, is admitted by all fair-minded persons to be of such a nature that it would satisfy any intelligent jury that I was not only wrongfully found guilty of murder, but was most wrongfully treated by Mr. Matthews. It completely exonerates me from the charge of murder as well as "administering and attempting to administer arsenic." Since this evidence was published, no one has attempted to justify the conviction or the sentence passed upon me.

Had the jury, instead of finding a verdict of "guilty" of murder, returned a verdict in the same terms as the finding of Mr. Matthews, the judge must have entered it as "not guilty" and discharged me.

Lord Russell's Letter

Well might the Lord Chief Justice Russell of Killowen write me, as he did on the 27th of June, 1895, telling me that he had never relaxed his efforts to urge my release, and saying:

Royal Court, 27th June, 1895.

Mrs. Maybrick,

Dear Madam. I have been absent on circuit; hence my delay in answering your letter.

I beg to assure you that I have never relaxed my efforts where any suitable opportunity offered to urge that your release ought to be granted. I feel as strongly as I have felt from the first that you ought never to have been convicted, and this opinion I have very clearly expressed to Mr. Asquith, but I am sorry to say hitherto without effect.

Rest assured that I shall renew my representations to the incoming Home Secretary, whoever he may be, as soon as the Government is formed and the Home Secretary is in a position to deal with such matters.

I am,

Faithfully,

Russell of Killowen.

This also seems to be the opinion of the leading counsel for the prosecution, Mr. Addison, Q.C., M.P. (now Judge Addison, of the Southwark County Courts), who is reported to have said, after the summing up, that "the jury could not, especially in view of the medical evidence, find a verdict of guilty." This statement will be found in Sir Charles Russell's protest to Mr. Matthews.

Efforts for Release

The public are not probably fully aware how much intensity of feeling and earnest work has been expended on my case during the fourteen and one-half years of my imprisonment. The Home Office knows. Men in high positions in both political parties in England have often united in demanding a new trial. The almost invariable reply has been that the best means to effect my release was to obtain new facts or evidence, and submit these to the Home Secretary for his consideration. Those well-meaning advisers seemed to forget that the half million of petitioners for my reprieve or free pardon in England—not to count those in America—were not moved thereto by new facts or evidence, but by the absence of facts or evidence sufficient to prove that the alleged crime had been committed by any one, or that either guilt or complicity in that crime, if crime it were, attached to me. Surely it is not the business of the public nor of individual citizens to prove the innocence of any unhappy person whom process of law selects for punishment, while it is the business of every citizen to see that the courts incontestably prove the guilt of any person accused of a crime before sentence is passed, in the following manner:

1. It must be proved that a crime has been committed.

2. It must be proved beyond a reasonable doubt that the accused person is the one who committed it.

Even New Evidence Superfluous

Neither condition has yet been fulfilled in my case. The evidence on which a half million petitioners said and say I was unjustly condemned is sufficient in itself. While it is true if a new trial had been granted me I could have produced new evidence that overwhelmingly demonstrated my innocence, it is also true that more facts or new evidence were not requisite to enable justice to be done.

The Doctors' Doubt

The doctors who gave evidence in favor of death by arsenical poisoning all stated that they would not have felt certain on the subject if the one-tenth of a grain of arsenic had not been found in the body. Therefore, since the presence of that arsenic could be otherwise accounted for, I was entitled to an acquittal even on the evidence of the Crown medical witnesses. Moreover, the symptom on which two or three doctors for the prosecution laid most stress—continuous vomiting—was referred by the third to morphia administered by himself. All three were examined before any evidence of Mr. Maybrick's habit of arsenic taking was given. Had they believed him to be an arsenic eater, they might have arrived at a different conclusion. The doctors for the defense, who declared that Mr. Maybrick's symptoms were not those of arsenical poisoning, were men of far more experience as regards poisons than the Crown medical witnesses. The quantity of arsenic found in the body was, in their opinion, quite consistent with administration in medicinal doses, and might have been introduced a considerable time before.

The proved administration of poison with intent to kill is punishable by penal servitude, but not necessarily for life—sometimes for only three years; but the charge must be proved in open court to be a felonious attempt by some means actually used to effectuate the intent, and it remains with the prosecution to produce the necessary evidence that the means used were sufficient for the accomplishment of the effect.

The medical evidence proved that the quantity of arsenic—one-tenth of a grain—found in Mr. Maybrick's body was not sufficient to have produced death.

Public Surprise at Verdict

The Times of August 8, 1889, declared that, of the hundreds of thousands of persons who followed the case with eager interest and attention, not one in three was prepared for the verdict. The large majority had believed that, in the presence of such contradictory evidence, the jury would give the prisoner the benefit of the doubt and bring in a verdict as much like the Scotch "not proven" as is permitted by English law.

Character of Jury

There was strong prejudice against me, due to the numerous false and sensational reports circulated by the press during the interval between the arrest and the trial. The jury belonged to a class of men who were not competent to weigh technical evidence, and no doubt attached great

The jury was composed of three plumbers, two farmers, one milliner, one wood-turner, one provision dealer, one grocer, one ironmonger, one house-painter, and one baker weight to the opinions of the local physicians, one of whom was somewhat of a celebrity. But the main element in the conviction was Justice Stephen, whose mind, undoubtedly owing to incipient insanity (he died insane a year later), was incapable of dealing with so intricate a case.

The "Mad Judge"

The Liverpool Daily Post, as I am told, had been hostile rather than favorable toward me, but, on the death of Lord Chief Justice Russell, that journal, in articles of August 13 and 14, 1900, showed that it fully appreciated the unfairness of my trial, for it stated that no human being ought to be handed over to be tried by a "mad judge." The following is taken from The Post of August 13, 1900:

"The death of the Lord Chief Justice may have recalled to the minds of some Liverpool folk a sad and sordid tragedy enacted among them eleven years ago, in which he was a principal performer. I o those who were there, a vivid recollection still persists of that bright July morning when a thronged court, hushed in expectancy, awaited the beginning of the Maybrick trial. In fancy one still hears the distant fanfare of the trumpets as the judges with quaint pageantry passed down the hall, and still with the mind's eye sees the stately crimson-clad figure of the great mad judge as he sat down to try his last case. A tragedy, indeed, was played upon the bench no less than in the dock.

"Few who looked upon the strong, square head can have suspected that the light of reason was burning very low within; yet as the days of the trial dragged by—days that must have been as terrible to the judge as to the prisoner—men began to nod at him, to wonder, and to whisper. Nothing more painful was ever seen in court than the proud old man's desperate struggle to control his failing faculties. But the struggle was unavailing. It was clear that the growing volume of facts was unassorted, undigested in his mind; that his judgment swayed backward and forward in the conflict of testimony; that his memory failed to grip the most salient features of the case for many minutes together. It was shocking to think that a human life depended upon the direction of this wreck of what was once a great judge."

Justice Stephen's Biased Charge

The charge of Mr. Justice Stephen to the jury positively teemed with misstatements as to the evidence given during the trial. I quote a statement from the same journal in its issue of August 17, 1900:

"I should be very sorry to think that the same number of errors as to the matters of fact given in the evidence had ever been made in any judge's charge. It simply swarms with them, and as the jury at the end of a long trial is likely to prefer the judge's resume to their own recollection, I doubt if the verdict in the Maybrick case was founded on the evidence at all. And if I am right in thinking that the jurors founded their verdict on the judge's recapitulation of the evidence rather than on the evidence itself, I do not see how any counsel could have saved the prisoner."

That the jury "did not hear the whole of the evidence very distinctly" is admitted by one of them in the Liverpool Daily Post of August 10, 1889. Consequently they were likely to be unduly influenced by the judge's charge. There is no evidence that the jury detected the judge's misstatements, as a more intelligent jury certainly would have done. Their minds were "taken captive" by the charge of Justice Stephen, and they were as "clay in the hands of the potter."

Lord Russell's Memorandum Quashed

The Lord Chief Justice sent the Home Secretary a memorandum consisting of twenty folios, in which he stated the strong opinion that "Mrs. Maybrick ought to be released at once." The Lord Chief Justice also requested that the contents of his memorandum be made public. Yet when asked in the House of Commons to lay the document on the table of the House in order that it might be accessible to the members, the Home Secretary emphatically declined. The London Daily Mail, in a leader on this incident, said:

"The only conceivable reasons for declining to give publicity to the letter, which was actually intended for publication, are apparently official red tape and the fear of giving new life to the agitation in favor of Mrs. Maybrick's release. This result will be almost as effectually achieved by surrounding the case with further mystery and leaving upon the public mind the grave suspicion that justice may not have been done."

Repeated Protests of Lord Russell

The following extracts are taken from the "Life of Lord Russell of Killowen" by R. Barry O'Brien.

"In November, 1895, he [Lord Russell] wrote to Sir Matthew White-Ridley, conveying his strong and emphatic opinion that Florence Maybrick ought never to have been convicted; that her continued imprisonment is an injustice which ought promptly to be ended, and added: 'I have never wavered in this opinion. After her conviction I wrote and had printed a memorandum, which I presume is preserved at the Home Office. Lest it should not be, I herewith transmit a copy.'

"As is known, what happened was that Mr. Matthews, after consultation with the present Lord Chancellor, Lord Salisbury, and Mr. Justice Stephen, and after seeing Dr. Stephenson, the principal Crown witness, and also the late Dr. Tidy, respited the capital sentence on the expressed ground that there was sufficient doubt whether death had been caused by arsenical poisoning to justify the respite.

"It will be seen (1) that such a doubt existed as to the commission of the offense for which Florence Maybrick was tried as rendered it improper, in the opinion of the Home Secretary and his advisers, that the capital sentence should be carried out; and (2) that for more than six years Florence Maybrick has been suffering imprisonment on the assumption of Mr. Matthews that she committed an offense for which she was never tried by the constitutional authority and of which she has never been adjudged guilty."

From page 261: "This is in itself a most serious state of things. It is manifestly unjust that Florence Maybrick should suffer for a crime in regard to which she has never been called upon to answer before any lawful tribunal.

"Is it not obvious that if the attempt to murder had been the offense for which she was arraigned, the course of the defense would have been different? I speak as her counsel of what I know. Read the report of the defense, and you will see that I devoted my whole strength to and massed the evidence upon the point that the prosecution had misconceived the facts, that the foundation on which the whole case rested was rotten, for that, in fact, there was no murder; that, on the contrary, the deceased had died from natural causes.

"It is true that incidental reference was made to certain alleged acts of Florence Maybrick, but the references were incidental only; the stress of my argument being, in fact, that no murder had been committed^ because the evidence did not warrant the conclusion that the deceased had died from arsenical poisoning; On the other hand, had the Crown counsel suggested the case of attempt to murder by poison, it would have been the duty of counsel to address himself directly and mainly to the alleged circumstances which, it was argued, pointed to guilty intent. That these alleged circumstances were capable in part of being explained, in part of being minimized, and in part of being attacked as unreliably vouched, cannot, I think, be doubted by any one who has with a critical eye scanned the evidence. I do not deny that my feelings are engaged in this case. It is impossible that they should not be, but I have honestly tried to judge the case, and I now say that if I was called upon to advise in my character' of head of the Criminal fudicature of this country, I should advise you that Florence Maybrick ought to be allowed to go freed

From page 262: "I think it my duty to renew my protest against the continued imprisonment of Florence Maybrick. I consider the history of the case reflects discredit on the administration of the criminal law. I think my protest ought to be attended to at last. The prisoner has already undergone punishment for a period four times as long, or more, as the minimum punishment fixed by law for the commission of the crime, of which she has never been convicted or for which she has never been tried, but for which she has been adjudged guilty by your predecessor in the office of Home Secretary."

The American Official Petition

The following is quoted from the American Official Petition sent to the Rt. Hon. Henry Matthews, Q.C., M.P., Her Majesty's principal secretary for the Home Department:

"As Florence Elizabeth Maybrick is an American woman, without father, brother, husband, or kin in England, except two infant children, enduring penal servitude for life in Woking Prison;

"As the conduct of her trial resulted in a profound impression of a miscarriage of justice, in an earnest protest against the verdict, and the execution of the sentence of death, and its commutation to penal servitude for life on the ground of reasonable doubt whether a murder had been committed;

"As a careful legal scrutiny of the evidence given at the trial by eminent solicitors, barristers, queen's counsel, and members of Parliament, and the production of facts not in evidence at the trial have resulted in a final decision of counsel that the case is one proper for the grave consideration of a criminal appellate tribunal—if such a tribunal existed;

"Therefore, we earnestly ask that the Rt. Hon. Henry Matthews, Q.C., M.P., Her Majesty's principal secretary of state for the Home Department, will advise Her Majesty to order the pardon and release of the prisoner, who has now suffered an imprisonment of three years.

"Levi P. Morton, Vice-President of the United States, President of the Senate.
"Charles T. Crisp, Speaker of the House of Representatives.
"Charles Foster, Secretary of the Treasury.
"James G. Blaine, Secretary of State.
"S. B. Elkins, Secretary of War.
"W. FI. Miller, Attorney-General.
"John Wanamaicer, Postmaster-General.
"B. T. Tracy, Secretary of the Navy.
"John B. Noble, Secretary of the Interior.
"G. M. Rusk, Secretary of Agriculture.
"J., Cardinal Gibbons.
"J. M. Scofield, Major-General Commanding the Army.

"A. W. Truly, Brigadier-General-in-Chief, Signal Office.

"Thomas Lincoln Casey, Brigadier-General-in-Chief of Engineers.

"Joseph Cabell Breckenridge, Brigadier-General, Infantry-General.

"J. O. Kelton, Brigadier-General, Adjutant-General.

"William Smith, Paymaster-General.

"H. M. Batchelder, General Quartermaster-General.

"B. DuBarry, General and Commanding General Infantry.

"O. Sutherland, General Infantry General.

"D. W. Flagler, Chief of Ordnance.

"J. Norman Lisber, Acting Judge-Advocate-General.

"Thomas Ewing, Brevet-Major-General, U. S. A., and many others."

Secretary Blaine's Letter to Minister Lincoln

I will conclude by quoting the letter of Secretary Blaine to Mr. Robert Lincoln [son of Abraham Lincoln], then Minister to the Court of St. James. It will be seen that Mr. Blaine was of opinion that I had lost my citizenship. Since this letter was written it has been decided by the Supreme Court of the United States that a woman married to a foreigner, on the death of her husband can, on application, be reinstated to citizenship.

"Department of State, Washington,

"March 7, 1892.

"My dear Mr. Lincoln: As Mrs. Maybrick lost her American citizenship by her English marriage, and as I fear she does not resume it by her widowhood, I cannot instruct you officially as to the course you should pursue toward her.

"But her American and Southern birth, her connection with many families of the highest respectability and even of prominence in the country's service, have attracted much attention to her fate.

"I have no other interest in her than an interest which you and I share in common with all our countrymen—the desire to help an American woman in distress. That she may have been influenced by the foolish ambition of too many American girls for a foreign marriage, and have descended from her own rank to that of her husband's family, which seems to have been somewhat vulgar, must be forgiven to her youth, since she was only eighteen at the time of her marriage.

"There is a wide and widening belief in this country that she is legally innocent and illegally imprisoned. The official charge of the judge that murder must be proved and the official announcement of the Home Secretary that the evidence leaves a 'reasonable doubt' of murder are the premises of but one conclusion—the discharge of the prisoner.

"The fact that she was never indicted or tried by a jury of her peers on a specific count of felonious attempt to administer arsenic, yet is condemned to penal servitude for life on the Home Secretary's statement that she evidently made such an attempt, can never be reconciled to the English principle that an accused person shall be tried by a jury of his peers. Lawyers here are among the strongest believers in the illegality of her imprisonment. Indeed, the sense of injustice is developing and deepening into horror.

"Officially I could only instruct you on behalf of a multitude of American citizens to investigate her case. Personally I beg to express to you my deep interest in it, and pray you, if possible, to communicate with Messrs. Lumley and Sir Charles Russell as to any method of American cooperation which may seem to them desirable.

"Messrs. Lumley have made a very able brief, which I am sure would interest you, and which seems to me unanswerable. Sir Charles Russell, whose reputation you know, is her counsel. Consult with them what best can be done, from an American point of view, to secure Mrs. Maybrick's release. And if you shall have read Lumley's brief, I am sure that conviction will lead you to personal activity in her behalf.

"You can communicate with me in strict confidence, as from one American citizen to another, for the relief of an American woman helplessly enduring a great wrong.

"Believe me, etc.,

"James G. Blaine."

And yet it required the time from March 7, 1892, until July 20, 1904, to attain my liberation; and then it was accomplished by time limit and by no act of grace or concession on the part of the English Government.

"Why he lacked the courage of his convictions can only be surmised. At all events he did not dare to take the responsibility of allowing her to be executed.

"The intercession of the American Government through Mr. Blaine, Secretary of State, was urgent, strong, and most intense. It is incredible that Mr. Matthews desired any loophole to release her. The case was full of them.

"Sir Matthew White-Ridley was not a lawyer, and there is no probability that he ever read the evidence in the case, which was voluminous. He could not have read the papers in three days if he had attempted it. He simply followed his predecessor's line and was not able to take up the case on its merits."

Lord Russell's Conviction of Mrs. Maybrick's Innocence

This statement of Mr. Lucy is of great value as an answer to the assault made on Lord Russell's memory after his death, on his firm belief in my innocence.

Lord Hugh Cecil wrote to a constituent:

"I believe I am right in stating that he (Lord Russell) never said that he believed Mrs. Maybrick to be innocent."

When this was shown Lord Russell by Mr. A. W. McDougall, Esq., the Chief Justice exclaimed:

"Does Lord Hugh Cecil suppose that I would abandon all the traditions of the Bar and put forward publicly as an argument in such a case my personal belief in this, that, or the other thing? Does he suppose that I would have made all the efforts I have been making to obtain her freedom if I believed her to be guilty?"

Explanation of Attitude of Home Secretaries

"Personal Rights," of November 15, in commenting on the statement of Mr. Lucy in The Strand Magazine, says:

"We do not share the belief that Sir Fitz-James Stephen was insane in any plenary sense at the time of the trial; but we are convinced that he was not fully sane. His charge to the jury, the report of which is reproduced in full in Mr. Levy's book, is grotesquely inaccurate; and if the jury took it to be a compendium of the evidence—as they probably did—the result of their deliberation is fully accounted for. Indeed, if the facts were such as the judge stated, the verdict could hardly be impugned. How different they were may be seen by any one who compares the evidence with the judge's charge, in the book already referred to. To take a single instance: the judge stated that, according to the evidence of Alice Yapp, at the commencement of Mr. Maybrick's illness, he was very sick and in great pain immediately after some medicine was given to him by his wife. Alice Yapp swore nothing of the kind. She saw neither any administration of medicine nor any sickness. We could give other instances of gross inaccuracy, generally leading to the conclusion of the prisoner's guilt; but, for our present purpose, the above incident will suffice.

"If this was the character of the judge's charge to the jury, what confidence can be placed in his notes? Still upon those notes was probably based the conclusions of successive Home Secretaries or of the officials employed by them. When Mr. Lucy holds up his hands in astonishment at the marvelous consensus of opinion of various Home Secretaries, he seems to us to manifest remarkable blindness—for one so long behind the Speaker's chair—as to the vicarious nature of that opinion. It is more than possible that the conclusions of Mr. Matthews, Mr. Asquith, and Sir Matthew White-Ridley were all drawn for them by the same gentleman, or, at least, that the same gentleman helped these various Home Secretaries to come to the same conclusion.

"We hope that Mr. Ritchie, the new Home Secretary, will judge this matter for himself. Let him read the salient portions, at least, of Mr. Levy's book, and, per contra, the article of X. Y. Z. in The Contemporary Review of September last. If he likes to make the inquiry, he will find that X. Y. Z. is one of his new permanent staff, and that the doctrines put forward in the article are the embodiment of Home Office practise. This is a matter which does not concern the Maybrick case alone. Scarcely a month passes without some new manifestation of injustice brought about by adherence to the traditions of the department over which Mr. Ritchie now presides. If he will seek out this hydra and slay it, he will leave for himself an immortal name among Secretaries of State, and—what he will hold of more importance—he will cut off a permanent source of injustice, give releasement and joy to the innocent pining in prison, and breathe a new life into a department which is sadly in need of a renovating spirit."

Upholding the Justiciary

In the same number of this journal is an article from "Lex," a well-known writer in English journals, which we reproduce:

"Sir: May I call attention to the two articles in the Liverpool Post of August 13 and 14, in which the utter incompetence of the judge at the Maybrick trial is strongly asserted? The writer is distinctly hostile to the prisoner, and writes without any intention of raising the question whether the trial was not null and void; but as the English system consists of trial by judge and jury, the total incompetence of either element should clearly vitiate it. Moreover, Mr. Ruggles-Brise, on the occasion of a visit to America in 1897, stated that the reason of the steadfast refusal of *the Home Secretary to release the prisoner was his desire to uphold the wholesome authority of the English justiciary.* That authority cannot be regarded as wholesome if the judge was insane. Lord Russell, who was present throughout the trial, was of different opinion from that of the judge. He was undoubtedly sane. If Sir J. F. Stephen was insane, the public will, I think, be of opinion that the sane judge should have had the most influence with the executive."

Need of Court of Criminal Appeal

Lord Esher, in The Times of August 17, 1889, strongly advocated a court of criminal appeal, and The Times, in an article of the same date, supported the views expressed by Lord Esher and by Lord Fitzgerald, as follows:

"A court of appeal, as Lord Esher sketches it, would not be open to the objections which can be fairly urged against our present informal method of procedure. The Home Secretary, as a quasi court of appeal, is, as Lord Fitzgerald remarks, not a judge and has not the power of a judge.... The judgment pronounced by a strong court of criminal appeal, such as Lord Esher's letter suggests, would do more to satisfy the public mind than the best efforts of the Home Secretary could possibly do. The reform which Lord Esher advocates has been long called for, and Lord Fitzgerald did well to press it on the Government.... What the public feel is that they would rather have the fallibility of trained judges than the fallibility of an individual sitting without any of the apparatus with which a court of law is enabled to detect truth from falsehood, and perhaps unconsciously confusing the prerogative of mercy with justice."

THE BRIEF OF MESSRS. LUMLEY & LUMLEY

THIS brief of Messrs. Lumley & Lumley, characterized in the preceding letter of Secretary Blaine as "very able" and "unanswerable," is too long for reproduction in these pages in its entirety, and hence only the main points are given. The document was prepared at the instance of Lord Russell of Killowen for submission to himself and three other Queen's Counsel, with a view of obtaining a new trial. It may interest the reader to know that the money required to make this searching analysis by Messrs. Lumley & Lumley was raised by a popular subscription in America, through the good offices of the New York World. The eminent Queen's counsel, after a full consideration of the analysis of the case, submitted the following opinion:

Opinion—Re F. E. Maybrick

"Having carefully considered the facts stated in the elaborate case submitted to us by Messrs. Lumley & Lumley, and the law applicable to the matter, we are clearly of opinion that there is no mode by which in this case a new trial or a 'venire de novo' can be obtained, nor can the prisoner be brought up on a 'habeas corpus,' with the view to retrying the issue of her innocence or guilt.

"We say this notwithstanding the case of Regina vs. Scarfe (17 Q. B., 238, 5; Cox, C. C., 243; 2 Den., C. C., 281).

"We are of opinion that in English criminal procedure there is no possibility of procuring a rehearing in the case of felony where a verdict has been found by a properly constituted jury upon an indictment which is correct in form. This rule is, in our opinion, absolute, unless circumstances have transpired, and have been entered upon the record, which, when there appearing, would invalidate the tribunal and reduce the trial to a nullity by reason of its not having been before a properly constituted tribunal. None of the matters proposed to be proved go to this length.

"We think it right to add that there are many matters stated in the case, not merely with reference to the evidence at and the incidents of the trial, but suggesting new facts, which would be matters proper for the grave consideration of a Court of Criminal Appeal, if such a tribunal existed in this country.

(Signed) "Charles Russell, O.C.

"I. Fletcher Moulton, O.C.

"Harry Bookin Poland, Q.C.

"Reginald Smith, O.C.

"Lincoln's Inn, 12th April, 1892."

This opinion was based upon the following points, presented by Messrs. Lumley & Lumley:

Justice Stephen's Misdirections

The misdirections which are selected for consideration may be conveniently classed, among others, under these headings:

1. As to the facts disclosed in the evidence of the procuring and possession of arsenic by Mrs. Maybrick and of her administering it.

2. As to the cause of death.

A perusal of the summing-up from beginning to end impresses the mind with the feeling that, whenever Mr. Justice Stephen approached any fact offered by the defense which threw light upon the possession and an alleged administration of arsenic by Mrs. Maybrick, he drew the minds of the jury away from it; he played, in fact, the part of the peewit, which swoops and screams in another part of the field on purpose to hide where its nest is, and to draw the attention of the passers-by from the right spot.

Mr. Justice Stephen pointed out to the jury in his summing-up: "You must begin the whole subject of poison with this, which is a remarkable fact in the case and which it seems to me tells favorably rather than otherwise for the prisoner. You must take notice of it and consider what inference you draw from it. In the whole case, from first to last, there is no evidence at all of her having bought any poison, or definitely having had anything to do with procuring any, with the exception of flypapers. But there is evidence of a considerable quantity having been found in various things, which were kept some here and some there—kept principally, as I gather, in the inner room.... There is evidence about a considerable quantity of poison in this house, and more particularly about one or two receptacles which were in the inner room, Mr. Maybrick's dressing-room, as it has been pointed out."

Misdirection as to Mr. Maybrick's Symptoms

From the testimony it appears that on the 27th of April James Maybrick, before starting to the Wirrall Races, was sick. There is no actual evidence of vomiting, but he is described as sick, and as feeling a numbness in his legs while walking downstairs, which was an old standing complaint of his of many years. Both he himself and Mrs. Maybrick told the servants that this was due to a double dose of some London medicine. He got wet through at the races and dined in his wet clothes at a friend's (Mr. Hobson), on the other side of the Mersey, and did not return home till after the servants had retired to bed; but the next morning, Sunday, the 28th of April, he was taken ill, and Mrs. Maybrick sent a servant off hurriedly for Dr. Humphreys, who had not attended her husband before, but who was the doctor living nearest the house, and in the meantime got some mustard and water, telling him to take it, as it would remove the brandy at all events. Dr. Humphreys attended James Maybrick on the 28th, but was not told by him that he had vomited the day before.

Mr. Justice Stephen, when referring to 267 this, said: "The Wirrall Races were followed by symptoms which were described to be arsenical." It is submitted that this was a misdirection, the symptom there referred to being sickness, and there was no evidence of vomiting on any of the days immediately succeeding the Wirrall Races. But on the 28th of April the mustard and water was given him by Mrs. Maybrick for the purpose of producing sickness and removing the brandy, and if he had been sick it would have been attributable to mustard and water, not to arsenic.

On the other hand, the medical evidence showed that gastro-enteritis might have been set up either by improper food or drink, or an excess of either; or, again, by such a wetting through as deceased got at the Wirrall Races. On the 8th of May Alice Yapp communicated to Mrs. Briggs and Mrs. Hughes her suspicions that James Maybrick's illness was due to Mrs. Maybrick poisoning him with fly-papers.

Misdirection as to Mrs. Maybrick's Access to Poisons

The purchase and soaking of fly-papers is the only direct evidence of the possession of arsenic in any form by Mrs. Maybrick, but the judge told the jury, and it is submitted it is a gross misdirection, that Mrs. Maybrick "undoubtedly had access to considerable quantities of arsenic in other forms," inasmuch as the only evidence as to such access was that after the death of James Maybrick these two women, Mrs. Briggs and Alice Yapp, who exhibited the most unfriendly feeling toward her, said they had found in the house certain stores of arsenic.

It is submitted for the serious consideration of counsel that the circumstances under which these two women produced these stores of arsenic are so suspicious as to justify the suggestion that that arsenic was not there before his death, and that Mrs. Maybrick never did have any access to it or knowledge of it at all. There was no evidence as to where or by whom this arsenic was obtained, nor was there any evidence that the police had made any effort to discover where, when, or by whom that arsenic was procured.

[Note.—How and when this arsenic may have been procured by Mr. Maybrick himself will appear further on as a part of the new evidence.]

The places in which arsenic was found were open and accessible to every one in the house, and no person gave any evidence that he or she had ever seen it in the house before these two women found it after death.

As regards the black powder (arsenic mixed with charcoal) and the two solutions of arsenic produced by Mrs. Briggs and Alice Yapp, Mr. Davies, the analyst, gave evidence that, when analyzing the contents of the various bottles, he had searched diligently and microscopically for any traces, and could find no trace of charcoal having been introduced into any of them. So this circumstantial evidence may be eliminated.

As regards white arsenic, also produced by these women, it must be observed that not only was it not shown that Mrs. Maybrick had purchased any, but it is submitted that the judge ought to have pointed out to the jury, as the fact is, that it would have been almost impossible for her or any woman to have obtained any white arsenic at all. No shopkeeper dare sell it to any one except to a medical man, and even then under the stringent restrictions of the Sale of Poison Act.

At the trial a wholesale druggist (Thompson, of Liverpool) gave evidence that James Maybrick constantly visited his cousin, who had been in his employment at his stores, where he could have obtained white arsenic from him-without any difficulty; and it will be observed that it was found in his hatbox.

It is a remarkable thing in this connection that, while Edwin Maybrick called the police in on Sunday night, and gave them the black solutions and white solutions which Mrs. Briggs had found on the Sunday morning, he did not give them the black powder which Alice Yapp had found on the night before; and, in fact, that Michael Maybrick did not give it to the police until Tuesday, the 14th.

It is also a remarkable fact that, although these black solutions and that white solution of arsenic and that solid arsenic which Mrs. Briggs had found, were not handed by the police to the analyst until several days afterward, and were therefore not known to be arsenic by anybody, yet Mrs. Briggs was able to inform Mrs. Maybrick on Tuesday, the 14th, as was testified to, that these bottles contained arsenic.

It is submitted that Mrs. Briggs could not have known that without some other means of knowledge than looking at them.

The importance of this misdirection of the judge as to the question of possession of arsenic by Mrs. Maybrick cannot be overstated. It was conclusively shown that no decoction of fly-papers or of the black powder was the source of the arsenic with which certain articles found in the house and office were said to be infected, because the analyst said he had searched for the fibers of the papers and for the charcoal, and could not find any traces of either. If Mrs.

Maybrick knew of the pure arsenic, why should she have bought the fly-papers, either for a cosmetic purpose or murder, and what should she have wanted with "poison for cats?"

Misdirection as to "Traces" of Arsenic

Out of the list submitted by the police, therefore, the only two things which could have been the source of the arsenic were the bottle of saturated solution, No. 10 in the Police List, and the bottle of solid arsenic, No ii in the Police List.

It may be observed that if all the arsenic or "traces" of the same, with which various things were said to be infected, were collected together, it would not constitute a fatal dose, the smallest fatal dose recorded being two grains, and this in the case of a woman, and surely not in the case of a person addicted to large doses of arsenic.

At the inquest Mr. Davies defined what he meant by the word "trace." He said: "It means something under 1/100 part of a grain. It does not mean something which I could not weigh, but something which I could not guarantee to be absolutely free from other things; but anything under 1/100 part of a grain I should not consider satisfactory. If I said distinct traces, I should say it meant something between 1/100 and 1/1000 part of a grain, while a minute trace is less than 1/1000 part of a grain." In reference to Reinsch's test which Mr. Davies used in these experiments, this passage occurs in Taylor's "Medical Jurisprudence," vol i., p. 268: "The mere presence of a gray deposit on pure copper affords no absolute proof of the presence of arsenic.

Bismuth, antimony, and mercury all yield deposits with Reinsch's test. The gray deposit of bismuth may easily be taken for arsenic." And again: "The errors into which the faulty methods of applying Reinsch's test lead have led its reliability to be much discredited, and, although in skilful hands the results are trustworthy, it would be perhaps unsafe to rely upon it in an important criminal investigation."

It is submitted that the evidence relating to the articles which Mr. Davies said were infected with arsenic only to the extent of an unweighable trace could not and ought not to be regarded as proof that any arsenic at all was there, or as being anything more than a suspicion upon this analyst's mind that what he saw was arsenic, and that it was a misdirection on the part of Mr. Justice Stephen to treat a mere expression of opinion of that kind as proof of the presence of arsenic.

Misdirection as to Arsenic in Solution

It will be observed that the only things of which James Maybrick could have partaken [but did not], in which arsenic in a weighable form was present, were the bottle of Valentine's meat juice and the pot of glycerin, and that the arsenic found in them was found in a state of solution.

As regards the half grain of arsenic found in the meat juice, scientific evidence will be forthcoming that it is a physical impossibility for any person to dissolve half a grain of solid arsenic in 411 grains of Valentine's meat juice, which is all the liquid that was in the bottle when it was handed to Mr. Davies.

Mr. Davies, moreover, found that (although he used very loose and unscientific language in his evidence) the specific gravity of the meat juice was considerably reduced, thereby showing that the half grain of arsenic found in it had been introduced in the form of arsenic in solution.

It will now be observed that the only arsenic in solution which was available, among the stores of arsenic found in the house, was the bottle No. 10 in the police list, and it is submitted that bottle No 11 (solid arsenic) must, like the black solutions, be eliminated from any store of arsenic which Mrs. Maybrick, whether she had access to it or not, could have employed for the purpose of infecting any of the things found in the house to be infected.

Mr. Davies described the bottle No. 10 as a saturated solution of white arsenic, and he stated that it had been dissolved with water, some of the crystals remaining at the bottom undissolved.

At the inquest he stated, in reply to a question by the coroner: "The bottle No 10, which was also in the box, contained a saturated solution of arsenic and solid arsenic at the bottom. There was no label on it. It contained, solid and liquid, perhaps two grains—a grain at all events."

So it is evident that there was not a fatal dose even in the stores which Mrs. Maybrick could have used had she had access to it.

As regards this bottle, Mr. Justice Stephen told the jury: "A saturated solution is a solution which has taken up as much arsenic as it can, the water becoming saturated with arsenic; the remainder of the arsenic is found at the bottom. In this case there was a saturated solution of arsenic in the water and a small portion of arsenic at the bottom. With regard to that these questions arise: What was it for? Who is wanting such a quantity of strong solution of arsenic? Who has put it there and how is it to be used? These are the questions, in the solution of which I cannot help you. There is nothing definite about it to connect Mr. Maybrick with it certainly. If he was in the habit of arsenic eating he would not keep it saturated in water in quantities he could not possibly use.

Later evidence showed that Mr. Maybrick secured as much as 150 grains from one person, only about two months before his death.

Mr. Davies found that this bottle "contained in solid and liquid perhaps two grains—a grain at all events." Now arsenic can be dissolved in water by two processes. In cold water by shaking it constantly for several hours (and the strongest solution that can be obtained by the cold-water process is a one-per-cent, solution, which is no stronger than the ordinary Fowler's solution as sold in the shops). That is called a "saturated solution" by the cold-water process. A solution of three or even four per cent, can be obtained with boiling water, but only when the water is kept on the constant boil for several hours; and that is also called a "saturated solution," so that the phrase "saturated solution" may mean either a weak solution of one per cent., such as is gained by the cold-water process, or a stronger solution of three per cent, by the boiling-water process, and Mr. Justice Stephen misdirected the jury as to the meaning of the phrase "saturated solution." He should have told them that a "saturated solution" of arsenic is one which has by any particular process taken up as much arsenic and retained it in solution, as is possible by that particular process, and that it might consequently be either a weak or a stronger solution, according as it has been dissolved by the cold-water or boiling-water process, by shaking for hours or boiling for hours.

The questions put to the jury by Mr. Justice Stephen upon the interpretation of the phrase "saturated solution" which he gave, namely, "How is it to be used?" "Who is wanting such a quantity of strong solution of arsenic?" are misdirections.

Mr. Clayton's Experiments

Counsel are referred to experiments made with solutions of arsenic by Mr. E. Godwin Clayton, of the firm of Hassall & Clayton. From these it will be seen that by the experiment there marked B, where the arsenic was shaken at intervals of twenty minutes for six hours, the result shows that it would require 186-1/2 grains of water to carry half a grain of arsenic. And that by experiment C, which is the strongest possible solution by the cold-water process, namely, one-per-cent, strength (equal to Fowler's solution), it would require 50 grains of water to carry half a grain, but to obtain this the arsenic has to be shaken with cold water at frequent intervals for four days.

Mr. Godwin Clayton, in his report as to these experiments, remarks: "I think, however, that as few people outside a chemical laboratory would have the patience or opportunity to make a solution by shaking it at short intervals during four days, the solution obtained in experiment B—namely, an arsenical strength of 0.268 per cent.—might be described in a popular sense, though not with strict scientific accuracy, as 'saturated solution of arsenic.'" But then if that be so, that is only about a quarter of the strength of Fowler's solution! The evidence of Mr. Davies as to the specific gravity of the meat juice being considerably reduced ought, it is submitted, not to have been received as scientific evidence, and it was a misdirection, to treat it as such, because without the slightest difficulty, as will be seen by a reference to Mr. Godwin Clayton's experiments, Mr. Davies's evidence ought to have been scientifically exact, because he could have shown that (for example) if a solution of the strength of experiment B had been used, the 411 grains of liquid would have contained 186-1/2 of solution of arsenic and 244-1/2 grains of meat juice; and, further, that the specific gravity of the meat juice would, in that case, have been lowered from 1.2143 to 1.1263; and it was, therefore, not only possible, but the duty of Mr. Davies, as an expert, to have shown, by comparing the specific gravity of the bottle No. 10 and the specific gravity of Valentine's meat juice, that the "arsenic in solution" which had been introduced into it had been introduced into it out of that particular bottle, No 10.

Then, again, it will be seen from these experiments of Mr. Godwin Clayton that if the solution in bottle No. 10 had been a strong hot-water solution of three per cent., the specific gravity would not have been considerably reduced, because the meat juice would in that case have contained only 15-1/2 grains of arsenical solution. To have obtained such a solution, the "arsenic powder" must have been boiled with distilled water for four hours; and it is submitted that it would have been impossible, in the first place, for Mrs. Maybrick, or any person outside a laboratory, to have adopted such a process of dissolving arsenic without the knowledge of the servants or anybody else; and, further, that even if she could have done this, she could not have possibly weighed out exactly half a grain of it, which is what Mr. Davies found; and it is suggested that the only way in which that half grain of arsenic could possibly have been measured into that bottle, must have been by introducing Fowler's solution, and no Fowlers solution was found in the house—and in no way was it suggested that Mrs. Maybrick had any access to any, though others in that house may have been able to procure such a medicinal dose of it.

Misdirection as to Arsenic in Glycerin

As regards the glycerin, Inspector Baxendale said he found this bottle in the lavatory on the 18th of May. There was no evidence that this bottle had ever been in Mrs. Maybrick's hands, and there was no evidence that any part of it had been used by James Maybrick. There was evidence that it was a freshly opened bottle. Scientific evidence will be forthcoming that it is an abolute impossibility for any person to distribute arsenic evenly through a pound of glycerin.

It is suggested that there is no possible means by which that glycerin could have been administered with a felonious intent to

James Maybrick; the mere moistening the lips with small quantities of it could not have operated in that way.

Scientific evidence will be forthcoming that glycerin, when kept in glass bottles, generally does contain arsenic, which it extracts from the glass of the bottle.

In 1888 Jahns drew attention to arsenic being present in glycerin.

In 1889 Vulpius also drew attention to it.

Siebold (see *Pharmaceutical Journal*, 5th October, 1889) said, at the Pharmaceutical Conference, on the 11th September, 1889, that his experiments were made with toilet and pharmaceutical glycerin, and that the majority showed presence of arsenious acid, varying from 1 grain in 4,000 to 1 grain in 5,000.

It may be pointed out that this is a larger quantity than Mr. Davies found, which was only "about Tl(T of a grain in 1,000 grains."

The evidence relating to the administration of glycerin was that of Nurse Gore and Nurse Callery, and was to the effect that on Thursday night they refreshed James Maybrick's mouth with glycerin and borax mixed in a saucer that was on the table in the sick-room, and that Mrs. Maybrick had brought the glycerin that was used either from the medicine cupboard in her room or from the washstand drawer.

The attention of counsel is called to the fact that this saucer of mixed glycerin and borax which was actually used was not produced at the trial, but Justice Stephen, when summing up to the jury, said: "Then you get the blue bottle which contained Price's glycerin. Here is the bottle, which there is no evidence to show that Mrs. Maybrick had even seen or touched; a considerable portion is still left. That glycerin was found in the lavatory outside, and if the bottle were filled and the same proportion of arsenic added, there would be two-thirds of a grain of arsenic in it. You have heard already that his mouth was moistened with glycerin and borax apparently the night before he died. If that be so, and the glycerin be really poison, it is certainly a very shocking result to arrive at." Sir Charles Russell: "I think the evidence of Nurse Gore is that the bottle that was used the night before was taken, not from the lavatory, but from the cupboard of the washstand." His Lordship: "It does not follow that that was the same bottle. One does not know the history of that bottle or where it went to. It may or may not have been the glycerin which was used for the purpose I have mentioned, namely, for moistening the lips. But it does appear in the case that a bottle was found in the lavatory, and that it contained a grain of arsenic, and that His mouth was moistened with glycerin and borax during the night in question; but the identity between that bottle and the bottle which contained the glycerin is not established and not proved."

It is submitted that the above was an unfair and inflammatory suggestion and amounts to a gross misdirection, especially after all the evidence about the condition of deceased's tongue and his complaining of a sensation as of a hair in his throat.

This concludes the whole of the evidence to any articles containing arsenic which were found in the house, in which the arsenic was present in anything except as unweighable "traces."

Misdirection as to Evidence of Physicians

Justice Stephen further summed up: "The witness (Dr. Stevenson) stated: 'I should say more arsenic was administered on the 3d of May.'" It will be seen, by a reference to Dr. Stevenson's evidence, that Dr. Stevenson did not say this.

Dr. Humphreys was the only medical man in attendance at that time. The only symptoms on Friday, the 3d, were that he had "vomited twice." At the inquest Dr. Humphreys said as to this:

O. "Did he say anything about his lunch on the previous day, Thursday, the 2d?"

A. "Yes; he said some inferior sherry had been put into it, and that it had made him as bad as ever again."

And that also appears in Dr. Stevenson's evidence at the trial:

"He told the doctor he had not been well since the previous day, when I learn he had his lunch at the office."

It cannot be suggested that the fact that the man vomited twice on Friday night was attributable to any arsenic taken at midday on Thursday, for Dr. Stevenson testified that the vomiting, which is a symptom of arsenic, usually follows the administration in about half an hour.

Dr. Carter, who was not called in to the patient until Tuesday, May 7th, in his evidence, however, suggested that:

"I judge that the fatal dose must have been given on Friday, the 3d, but a dose might have been given after that. When he was so violently ill on the Friday, I thought it would be from the effects of the fatal dose, but there might have been subsequent doses"; and in cross-examination he explained that he had made this suggestion about the fatal dose because: "I was told he was unable to retain anything on his stomach for several days."

It is submitted that the judge, when summing up, misdirected the jury by ignoring entirely the evidence and substituting for it this reckless suggestion of Dr. Carter's.

Misdirection as to Times When Arsenic May Have Been Administered

The only occasions on which it was possible to suggest any act of administration of arsenic were the medicine on the 27th of April and the food at the office on May 1st and May 2d; and the judge told the jury:

"The argument that the prisoner administered the arsenic is an argument depending upon the combination of a great variety of circumstances of suspicion. The theory is that there was poisoning by successive doses, and it is rather suggested that there may have been several doses. But I do not know that there was any effort made to point out the precise times at which doses may have been administered."

Under such circumstances it is submitted that the statement of the judge as to the medicine on the 27th of April, and as to the food at office, and as to the statement that " Friday (3d May) was the day on which began the symptoms of what may be called the fatal dose," are misdirections of vital importance to this case, and such as to entitle Mrs. Maybrick to have the verdict set aside and have a new trial ordered.

Misdirection as to Mrs. Maybrick's Changing Medicine Bottles

As regards the question of attempts to administer arsenic, the occasions upon which such conduct was imputed are changing medicine from one bottle into another and the Valentine's meat juice. As regards the changing the bottle, there were two occasions when evidence was given as to Mrs. Maybrick's doing this. The first was on the 7th of May, when Alice Yapp said that some of the medicines were kept on a table near the bedroom door and some in the bedroom, and that on Tuesday, 7th of May, she saw Mrs. Maybrick on the landing near the bedroom door, and what was she doing? She was apparently pouring something out of one bottle into another. They were medicine bottles.

That is the whole evidence as to the incident, and as all the bottles in the house were analyzed, and none found to contain even a trace of arsenic except the Clay and Abraham's bottle—which James Maybrick was not taking at that time—the judge could not properly direct the jury to regard it as a matter of suspicion; but he did do so. He referred to this incident thus:

"On the 28th April (the day after the Wirrall Races) Mrs. Maybrick sent for Dr. Humphreys, and afterward she was seen pouring medicine from one bottle into another."

It is submitted that this was a serious misdirection.

The other occasion was on Friday, the 10th of May, when Michael Maybrick, seeing Mrs. Maybrick changing a medicine from one bottle to another in the bedroom, took the bottles away and had the prescription made up again, saying: "Florrie, how dare you tamper with the medicine?" Mrs. Maybrick explained that she was only putting the medicine into a larger bottle because there was so much sediment. Nurse Callery was present and there was no concealment about what she was doing, and the bullying conduct of Michael was absolutely without any sort of justification. These bottles were analyzed and found to be harmless.

Mr. Justice Stephen turned this incident, which occurred on the afternoon before death, and after she had been prevented from attending on her husband, against Mrs. Maybrick, thus—quoting Michael's evidence: "In the bedroom I found Mrs. Maybrick pouring from one bottle into another and changing the labels, and I said, Florrie, how dare you tamper with the medicine? And Justice Stephen continued: "Verily, this was a strange—I don't say strange considering the circumstances—but dreadfully unwelcome remark to make to a lady in her own house, when she was in attendance on her husband, and something which showed the state of feeling in his mind, and must have attracted her attention." It is submitted that this was a misdirection.

Misdirection as to Administration with Intent to Kill

There was also an attempt by the prosecution to suggest an attempt to administer medicine, arising out of an occasion when James Maybrick said to her, "You have given me the wrong medicine again," from which it appears that on the Friday, the day before death, Mrs. Maybrick was not giving him anything at all, but was trying to get him to take some medicine from Nurse Callery, who was endeavoring to induce him to take it. This was one of the medicines ordered by Dr. Humphreys, and was found free from arsenic. The judge did not refer to this in his summing-up, but reference to it is introduced here because it exhausts the whole evidence, with the exception of the Valentine's meat juice incident, as to any suggestions or even of any occasions of attempt to administer, while Mr. Matthews advised the Queen that the evidence leads clearly to the conclusion that the prisoner administered and attempted to administer arsenic to her husband with intent to murder," which formed his ground for consigning this woman to penal servitude for life. No evidence, either of any act of administration or of any act of attempt to administer either with or without felonious attempt, was given at the trial, which possibly could have led any person to any such conclusion, with the single exception of the Valentine's meat juice; and as none of that was administered after it had been in Mrs. Maybrick's hands, the utmost that could be said of it (assuming that she did put any arsenic into it) is that it was an attempt to administer, either feloniously or otherwise.

It is submitted that the judge misdirected the jury as to this incident, in that he did not tell them that the mere evidence of an attempt to administer arsenic was not sufficient—that they must be satisfied that the attempt to administer was with a *mens rea* and with an intent to murder.

Exclusion of Prisoner's Testimony

Mrs. Maybrick voluntarily told her solicitors, Mr. Arnold and Mr. Richard Cleaver, directly she was arrested and even before the inquest, that she had, at her husband's urgent request, put a powder into a bottle of Valentine's meat juice, but that she did not know, until Mrs. Briggs informed her that arsenic had been found in a bottle of meat juice, that the powder she had put in was assumably arsenic. [At the trial both Mr. Richard and Mr. Arnold Cleaver, her solicitors, offered to give evidence to this effect, but Justice Stephen refused to admit it.] She also tried to tell

Mrs. Briggs the same thing, but the policeman stopped the conversation; and she also told it to her mother on her arrival. Mrs. Maybrick made no attempt at concealment about having put this powder in, although no one had seen her do it, and her solicitors, instead of relying as a line of defense on showing there was no "*mens rea*" in what she had done, kept back her account of what she had done. At the trial, however, after all the evidence for the prosecution had been concluded without a single witness speaking of her having put anything into anything, she insisted on telling the jury, as she had told her solicitors, that she did put a powder into a bottle of meat juice, in accordance with an urgent-request of her husband's, but that she did not know it was arsenic. If she did not know, there was no "*mens rea*." Upon that evidence, and upon certain suspicious circumstances connected with her conduct in taking the meat juice into the dressing-room and replacing it in the bedroom, the judge, as it is submitted, misdirected the jury in the following passage:

"Mr. Michael Maybrick says: Nothing was given to my brother out of that.' That is to say, nothing was given to him out of the bottle of Valentine's meat juice, which undoubtedly had arsenic in it. Its presence was detected, but of that bottle which was poisoned he certainly had none. He had a small taste of it before it was poisoned, given him by Nurse Gore."

It is submitted that the words "before it was poisoned" is a gross misdirection.

Misdirection as to Identity of Meat-Juice Bottle

It may be convenient here to interpose the following remarks on the subject of the identity of the bottle. Counsel will observe that the judge referred to the evidence at the inquest and at the magisterial inquiry, which, it is suggested, enables a reference to any discrepancies in the evidence of the witnesses on the three occasions—inquest, magisterial inquiry, and trial.

The identity of the half-used bottle, which was found to contain "half a grain of arsenic in solution," with the bottle which Mrs. Maybrick took into the dressing-room, was not proved. It was assumed alike by the prosecution and the defense, and by Mrs. Maybrick herself, but it was not proved. It was proved that there was another half-used bottle, of which James Maybrick had partaken on Monday, 6th of May, when Dr. Humphreys said:

"Some of the Valentine's meat juice had been taken, but it did not agree with the deceased and made him vomit. Witness did not remember him vomiting in his presence, but he complained of it. Witness told deceased to stop the Valentine's meat juice, and said he was not surprised at it making Mr. Maybrick sick, as it made many people sick."

There was, therefore, another half-used 300 bottle. The attention of counsel is strongly directed to the question of the identity of this half-used bottle.

Besides the one in which the arsenic was detected, there was another half-used bottle produced at the trial, which was found by Mrs. Briggs after death in one of James Maybrick's hatboxes in the dressing-room, together with the black solutions and white solutions of arsenic, and this bottle was found free of arsenic.

As to the bottle which Mrs. Maybrick had in her hands on the night of the 9th-10th of May, and which she took into the dressing-room, and as to which she volunteered the statement that she had put a powder in, as to which evidence was given by Nurse Gore, was thus voluntarily corroborated by Mrs. Maybrick in her statement to the jury. From this it appears that Nurse Gore, on her arrival for duty on Thursday night, opened a fresh bottle of meat juice, which had been given to her the night before by Edwin Maybrick, and gave the patient one or two spoonfuls, and then placed it on the table, from which she shortly afterward saw Mrs. Maybrick remove it and take it into the dressing-room, the door of which was not shut, and then return with it into the bedroom and replace it on the table. Nurse Gore thought she did this in a stealthy way. It must be remembered that Nurse Gore was naturally suspicious, as is shown by the fact that on two previous occasions she suggested suspicions with regard to changes in medicines by Mrs. Maybrick, which on analysis were proved to be free from arsenic. When the patient, a short time afterward, awoke, Mrs. Maybrick came into the bedroom again and removed the bottle from the table and placed it on the washstand, where there were only the ordinary jugs and basins, and there left it. Nurse Gore's usual suspicions were aroused and she gave the patient none of it, nor did Mrs. Maybrick ask her to give him any. When Nurse Gore was relieved by Nurse Callery the next morning (Friday, the 10th), at n o'clock, she called her attention to it and asked her to take a sample of it, which Callery did, and put it into an ordinary medicine bottle, which Nurse Gore gave her for the purpose. Nurse Gore left the bottle on the washstand where Mrs. Maybrick had placed it. Nurse Gore did not mention the circumstance to Dr. Humphreys when he came to see the patient at 8:30 a.m., nor to Michael Maybrick, whose attention she directed to a bottle of brandy instead, which on analysis was found harmless; and she then went into Liverpool and saw the matron, and on her return to the house at 2 o'clock told Callery to throw away the sample in accordance with the matron's orders, which Callery did. The bottle in which that sample was taken was not specially identified, though it must have remained on the premises. It ought to have been produced, because, if arsenic was detected in the sample, the bottle of Valentine's meat juice would have been identified by that means, and it would have been shown that the arsenic was in the meat juice which Mrs. Maybrick had taken into the dressing-room. On the other hand, as all the bottles which were in the house were analyzed and found free of arsenic, there is negative evidence that there was no arsenic in the sample taken.

Misdirection in Excluding Corroboration of Prisoner's Statement

Now the serious, most serious, consideration of counsel is asked for in comparing the evidence of these three witnesses—Gore, Callery, and Michael Maybrick—as given at the coroner's inquest, as it appears in the coroner's depositions, at the magisterial inquiry, as it appears in the magistrates' depositions, and as given at the trial. It will be seen that there are great discrepancies as to the place in the room from which Michael Maybrick took the half-used bottle in which Mr. Davies, the analyst, subsequently detected one-tenth of a grain of arsenic in solution. It is suggested that Mr. Michael's evidence at the inquest is the true account of where he got the bottle, and that his evidence at the trial is cooked, to suit the evidence of Gore, and that the identity of the bottle is not established. The statement, which in her statement to the jury Mrs. Maybrick said she was prevented by the policeman from making to Mrs. Briggs, the moment that person told her about arsenic being found in the meat juice, was communicated by Mrs. Maybrick at once to her solicitors, Mr. Arnold and Richard Cleaver; and it is submitted that it was a misdirection of the judge to exclude their evidence in corroboration of such a material and important fact in her favor, and a misdirection in refusing to allow corroboration in that way of what was in evidence, and did corroborate it—thereby constituting a matter which the jury should have had before them, as having a bearing on her statement.

Misdirections to Jury to Draw Illegal Inferences

The judge referred to the Valentine's meat-juice incident, the most vital point in the trial, in the following extraordinary manner at the end of his summing-up:

"I may say this, however: supposing you find a man dying of arsenic, and it is proved that a person put arsenic in his plate, and if he gives an explanation which you do not consider satisfactory—that is a very strong question to be considered—how far it goes, what its logical value is, I am not prepared to say—I could not say, and unless I had to write my verdict I should not say how I should deal with the verdict; but being no juryman, but only a judge, I can only say this, it is a matter for your serious consideration."

It is submitted that this was a gross misdirection and a cruel taunt to drive the jury into finding a verdict against the prisoner upon that ground, and it is submitted that so monstrously unfair an utterance cannot be found in the reports of any summing-up by any judge in any criminal case. See also another misdirection where the judge read the examination of Nurse Gore and omitted reference to the sample, but said of the bottle, "In point of fact, it remained where it was until taken away by Mr. Michael Maybrick," when it is in evidence that Nurse Callery had taken a sample of it during the eighteen hours it remained on the washstand, and that others beside Mrs. Maybrick had access to it.

It is submitted that, apart from the question of the identity of the bottle, there was no evidence, except Mrs. Maybrick's statement, that she had put anything into the bottle, which justified Mr. Justice Stephen in using the words, "He had a small taste of it before it was poisoned," inasmuch as, except Mrs. Maybrick's own voluntary statement that she had put a powder into a bottle of meat juice, there was nothing to show that the arsenic, detected by Mr. Davies in the bottle he analyzed, had not been in the bottle when Edwin Maybrick gave it to Nurse Gore and which she opened when she gave the patient "one or two spoonfuls."

Another misdirection in reference to the meat-juice incident will be found in the summing-up in the words:

"It has a sort of very remote bearing upon the statement which she made on Monday."

Instead of "a sort of very remote bearing," it was a matter of the greatest importance that it should be shown that at the very instant she heard that arsenic had been found in some meat juice, before even the inquest, and before any arsenic had been found in the body, she should have attempted to tell Mrs. Briggs that she had put a powder into some meat juice, but did not know what it was; and, in connection with this, the attention of counsel is called to the fact that Mr. Justice Stephen refused to allow evidence showing that she had made this statement from the very first.

Misdirections Regarding the Medical Testimony

As to the cause of James Maybrick's death, there was a most remarkable conflict of medical opinion. It was not until the post-mortem examination, held on Monday, the 13th of May, by Drs. Carter and Humphreys (the medical men who had attended the deceased during his illness), and Dr. Barron; that the cause of death was ascertained, and it was then found to be exhaustion, caused by gastroenteritis or acute inflammation of the stomach and intestines, which, in their opinion, had been set up by an irritant poison, but might have been set up by his getting wet through.

These doctors agreed that by the phrase "irritant poison" they meant any unwholesome food or drink.

Up to the time of death the doctors, Messrs. Humphreys and Carter, had supposed and treated the patient for dyspepsia, notwithstanding that suggestions had been made to them by Michael Maybrick that the patient was being poisoned; and they said in their evidence that but for the discovery of arsenic on the premises, they would have given a certificate of death from natural causes.

At the post-mortem examination they selected such portions of the body for analysis as they considered necessary, including, among other things, the stomach and its contents; and the analyst employed by the police (Mr. Davies) found no arsenic in the stomach or its contents, and was unable to discover any weighable traces of arsenic in any other portions of the body.

About three weeks afterward the body was, by order of the Home Secretary, exhumed, and fresh portions of it were taken for analysis, some of which were examined by Mr. Davies and other parts by Dr. Stevenson, one of the Crown analysts.

In those portions taken at the exhumation, the total result of the search for arsenic in the body was that Mr. Davies actually found unweighable arsenic, 2/100 a grain, in the liver, and Dr. Stevenson 76/100 of a grain in the liver and 15/100 in the intestines, making, when all added together, the total amount as found by Mr. Davies and Dr. Stevenson about one-tenth of a grain, made up of minute fractional portions of one-hundredths and one-thousandths.

It was shown in evidence that the smallest fatal dose of arsenic ever recorded was two grains, which was in the case of a woman, and who presumably was not an arsenic-eater.

It was shown in evidence that in the year 1888 Mrs. Maybrick had asked Dr. Hopper (who was at that time, and had been for many years, their regular medical attendant) to speak to Mr. Maybrick and prevent him taking certain medicines, which were doing him harm; that early in March she made the same appeal to Dr. Humphreys, suggesting at the time that Mr. Maybrick was taking a *white powder*, which she thought was strychnin.

At the magisterial inquiry Dr. Humphreys stated that Mrs. Maybrick had, on the occasion of his being called in to the patient on the 28th of April, also spoken to him about her husband taking this white powder, and that in consequence of this he asked Mr. Maybrick about taking strychnin and nux vomica.

Counsel will find proof, in the evidence given at the trial by Dr. Hopper, Mr. Heaton, Nicholas Bateson, Esq., Capt. Richard Thompson, Thomas Stansell, and Sir James Poole, ex-Mayor of Liverpool, as to the arsenic habit of James Maybrick and his opportunities for obtaining the drug. [To which must now be added the statutory declaration of Valentine Charles Blake, son of the late Sir Valentine Blake, M.P., that he, about two months prior to Mr. Maybrick's death, had procured him 150 grains of arsenic.] It may be stated here that from the appearance of the little bottles in which the white arsenic was found, they had been in use for a long time and were such as would be found as sample bottles in the offices of business houses to which it is unlikely Mrs. Maybrick would have access.

It is submitted that the discovery of such a tiny quantity of arsenic in the body of a man addicted to such extraordinary habits might reasonably be accounted for by those habits.

Conflict of Medical Opinion

The conflict of medical opinion which was exhibited on this trial arose upon the point as to whether arsenic had been the cause of the gastro-enteritis, of which it was admitted that the man died.

There was no conflict of medical opinion on the facts that the quantity found in the body was insufficient to cause death, nor that gastro-enteritis might be set up by a vast variety of things besides arsenic—in fact, by any impure food or by excessive alcohol or by getting wet through. It was shown in evidence that Mr. Maybrick got wet through at the Wirrall Races on the 27th of April, and that he afterward went in his wet clothes to dinner at a friend's on the other side of the Mersey.

The conflict of medical opinion amounted to this, that the Crown called Drs. Carter and Humphreys, who both admitted that they had never previously attended a case of arsenical poisoning, nor had ever before attended a post-mortem examination of a person whose death had been attributed to arsenic—in short, that they had had no experience whatever. The Crown also called Dr. Stevenson (who had not attended the deceased, but had conducted the analysis of parts of the body) as an expert in poisoning, and he said, as to the symptoms during life: "There is no distinctive diagnostic symptom of arsenical poisoning. The diagnostic thing is finding the arsenic."

The Crown also had Dr. Barron, who had attended the post-mortem, and who expressed himself unable to say that arsenic was the cause of the gastro-enteritis.

These witnesses, it may be observed, gave their evidence both as to the symptoms during life and as to the appearances at the post-mortem before the medical evidence for the defense had been called.

The witnesses called for the defense had none of them attended the deceased, but were called as experts in poisoning, viz., Dr. Tidy, a Crown analyst, Dr. Macnamara, and Professor Paul, who all gave positive evidence that neither the symptoms during life nor the appearance after death were such as could be attributed to arsenical poisoning; that, in fact, they pointed away from, instead of toward, arsenic being the cause of death.

The evidence of these witnesses was summarized very fairly by Mr. Justice Stephen.

In the face of such a conflict of medical opinion, it is submitted that Mr. Justice Stephen should have refused to allow the jury to return any verdict of guilty at all.

Misdirections as to Cause of Death

On the first day of his summing-up, however, Mr. Justice Stephen told the jury as to the law under which they were to return their verdict: "You have been told that if you are not satisfied in your minds about poisoning—if you think he died from some other disease—then the case is not made out against the prisoner. It is a necessary step—it is essential to this charge—that the man died of poison, and the poison suggested is arsenic. This is the question you have to consider, and it must be the foundation of a judgment unfavorable to the prisoner that he died of arsenic."

It is submitted that Mr. Justice Stephen misdirected the jury when he told them to satisfy their minds whether he died from any other disease, inasmuch as the only question before the jury was whether the cause of death was arsenic.

"The question for you is by what the illness was caused. Was it caused by arsenic or by some other means?"

It is submitted that that is a misdirection. It might have been put to a coroner's jury, but it was not a question which should have been put to a jury at a criminal trial.

It is submitted that he misdirected the jury in not also telling them that it was essential to a verdict unfavorable to the prisoner that the arsenic of which he died had been administered by her, and also in not telling the jury that it was essential to a verdict unfavorable to the prisoner that, if she had administered any, she had done it with intent to destroy life.

Misdirection to Ignore Medical Testimony

Mr. Justice Stephen then proceeded: "Now, let us see what the doctors say. Some say death was caused by arsenic, and others that it was not by arsenic—that he died of gastro-enteritis"; and he spoke of the medical evidence in a way which amounted to a direction to the jury that they were to treat it as tainted with subtle partizanship, and as evidence to which it was not necessary for them to attach serious importance. He, in fact, stated, and in so doing misdirected the jury, that though it was essential to a verdict unfavorable to the prisoner that he died of arsenic, that question was one which they, the jury, could come to their own opinion about, without taking into consideration the opinion of the medical experts, who had positively stated that arsenic was not the cause of death. In other words, he directed the jury that, as the medical experts could not agree that the cause of death was arsenical poisoning, it was for them to decide that question from their own "knowledge of human nature

On the second day of the summing-up the judge told the jury (and it is submitted that it contains gross misdirections): "You must consider the case as a mere medical case, in which you are to decide whether the man did or did not die of arsenic according to the medical evidence. You must not consider it as a mere chemical case, in which you decide whether the man died from arsenic which was discovered as the result of a chemical analysis. You must decide it as a great, high, and important case, involving in itself not only medical and chemical questions, but embodying in itself a most highly important moral question—and by that term, moral question, I do not mean a question of what is right and wrong in a moral point of view, but questions in which human nature enters and in which you must rely on your knowledge of human nature in determining the resolution you arrive at.

"You have, in the first place, to consider—far be it from me to exclude or try to get others to exclude from their own minds what I must feel myself vividly conscious of—the evidence in this matter. I think every human being in this case must feel vividly conscious of what you have to consider, but I had almost better say you ought not to consider, for fear you might consider it too much, the horrible nature of the inquiry in which you are engaged. I feel that it is a dreadful thing that you are deliberately considering whether you are to convict that woman of really as horribly dreadful a crime as ever any poor wretch who stood in the dock was accused of. If she is guilty—I am saying if my object is rather to heighten your feeling of the solemnity of the circumstances, and in no way to prevent you from feeling as you do feel, and as you ought to feel. I could say a good many other things about the awful nature of the charge, but I do not think it will be necessary to do any one thing. Your own hearts must tell you what it is for a person to go on administering poison to a helpless, sick man, upon whom she has already inflicted a dreadful injury—an injury fatal to married life; the person who could do such a thing as that must be destitute of the least trace of human feeling." And further on: "We have to consider this not in an unfeeling spirit—far from it—but in the spirit of people resolved to solve by intellectual means an intellectual problem op great difficulty 1'

Mr. Justice Stephen, in short, instead of putting to the jury for separate answers each of the following three questions:

1. Did this man die of arsenic?

2. Did Mrs. Maybrick administer that arsenic?

3. Did she do it feloniously? invited them to return a verdict of "guilty" or "not guilty" upon a direction of law, wherein he told them that they were to decide it as an intellectual problem, on the question which, it is submitted, can be formulated thus:

"Might this man have died of arsenic notwithstanding the opinion of the medical experts that he did not die of arsenic?" And the jury answered "Yes."

It is submitted that this was a gross misdirection.

It may be interesting and applicable to quote from a paper read by Sir Fitzjames Stephen himself at the Science Association in 1884: "It is not to be denied that, so long as great ignorance exists on matters of physical and medical science in all classes, physicians will occasionally have to submit to the mortification of seeing not only the jury, but the bar and bench itself, receive with scornful incredulity or with self-satisfied ignorance evidence which ought to be received with respect and attention." How prophetic this was as exemplified by his own attitude in this trial need not be pointed out.

Misreception of Evidence

Under the head of Misreception of Evidence may be classed the observations of the judge, where, apparently in order to prevent the jury from being influenced in favor of the prisoner, owing to the small quantity of arsenic found in the body of the deceased, he mentioned an instance of a dog being poisoned, in the body of which, though it had taken a large number of grains of arsenic, no arsenic was found after its death. The judge, in other words, turned himself into a witness for the prosecution. The unfairness to the prisoner of such a course is obvious. Had the judge been an ordinary witness he might have been cross-examined to show, e.g. that arsenic passes away from the body of a dog much more quickly than from that of a man, or that the circumstances as to time and quantity taken were such as to prove that there was no analogy between the two cases. As the matter stands, the judge's recollection of an experiment on a dog, which had been made many years before, was meant to rebut a proposition much relied on by the defense, viz., that the small quantity of arsenic found in the body of the deceased was consistent with the view that he was in the habit of taking arsenic, rather than with the case for the Crown that he had been intentionally poisoned.

Cruel Misstatement by the Coroner

The inquest was formally opened by taking the evidence of the identification of the deceased by his brother, Michael Maybrick, and then adjourned for a fortnight, the coroner announcing that there had been a post-mortem examination by Dr. Humphreys, and that the result of that examination was that poison was found in the stomach of the deceased in such quantities as to justify further examination; that the stomach of the deceased, and its contents, would meanwhile be chemically analyzed, and on the result of that analysis would depend the question whether or not criminal proceedings against some person would follow. Now the announcement that "poison had been found in the stomach of the deceased" was contrary to fact, and in consequence of this cruel misstatement the proceedings caused an immense amount of popular excitement and prejudice against the accused, who, being too ill to be removed, remained at Battlecrease House, in charge of the police, till the following Saturday morning, the 18th May, when a sort of court inquiry was opened in Mrs. Maybrick's bedroom by Colonel Bidwell, one of the county magistrates.

Medical Evidence for the Prosecution

The evidence of Dr. Arthur Richard Hopper, who had been Mr. and Mrs. Maybrick's medical adviser for about seven years, was taken. He had not attended Mr. Maybrick during his last illness, but spoke about Mrs. Maybrick having asked him the year before to check her husband from taking dangerous drugs, and that Mr. Maybrick had admitted to him that he used to dose himself with anything his friends recommended, and that he was used to the taking of arsenic.

Dr. Richard Humphreys spoke as to the symptoms of the illness and his prescriptions, and that he had not suspected poisoning until it was suggested to him and his colleague, Dr. Carter, and that he had himself administered arsenic to the deceased, in the form of Fowler's solution, on the Sunday or Monday before death, and that he refused a certificate of death only because arsenic had been found on the premises.

Dr. William Carter spoke of being called the Tuesday before death, and he agreed with Dr. Humphreys that an irritant poison, most probably arsenic, was the cause of death.

Dr. Alexander Barron gave evidence to the effect that he was unable to ascertain any particular poison.

Mr. Edward Davies, the analyst, was called, and gave evidence to the effect that he had found no weighable arsenic in the portions of the body selected at the post-mortem, but that he had subsequently found one fiftieth of a grain of arsenic in a part of the liver, nothing in the stomach or its contents, but traces, not weighable, in the intestines, and that he had found arsenic in some of the bottles and things found in the house after death and in the Valentine's meat juice.

The first issue which the jury at the trial had to determine was whether it was proved beyond reasonable doubt that the deceased died from arsenical poisoning.

Mr. Justice Stephen, in his summing-up, put this issue to the jury in the following words:

"It is essential to this charge that the man died of arsenic. This question must be the foundation of a verdict unfavorable to the prisoner, that he died of arsenic."

It must be assumed that this was a question exclusively for medical experts, notwithstanding which the judge, in summing up, told the jury:

"You must not consider this as a mere medical case, in which you are to decide whether the man did or did not die of arsenic poisoning according 10 the medical evidence. You must not consider it as a mere chemical case, in which you decide whether the man died from arsenic which was discovered as the result of a chemical analysis. You must decide it as a great and highly important case, involving in itself not only medical and chemical questions, but involving in itself a most highly important moral question'.'

Maybrick Died a Natural Death

Dr. Humphreys gave it as his opinion that the appearances at the post-mortem were consistent with congestion of the stomach not necessarily caused by an irritant poison, and that the symptoms during life were also consistent with congestion not caused by an irritant poison, but with acute inflammation of the stomach and intestines, produced by any cause whatever, and which would produce similar pathological results. He thought death was caused by some irritant poison, most likely arsenic, but he would not like to swear that it was. Dr. Humphreys' evidence, therefore, amounted to this, that the deceased died from gastro-enteritis, a natural disease, attributable to a variety of causes, and that, apart from the suggestions already referred to, he would have certified accordingly.

Dr. Humphreys' evidence was confirmed by that of Dr. Carter, who stated he came to the same conclusion as Dr. Humphreys, "but in a more positive manner." Dr. Carter had assisted at the post-mortem examination, besides being in close attendance on the deceased for the five days preceding his death, which he attributed to taking some irritant wine or decomposed meat, or to some grave error of diet; and when pressed as to whether he had any reason to suppose the article taken was poison, he explained that he did, but that by poison he meant something that was bad—it might be tinned meat, which the deceased had partaken of at the race dinner, or wine, or something which had set up gastritis. This witness's account of the post-mortem was that they pound no arsenic, but merely evidence of an irritant poison in the stomach and intestines, probably arsenic. Dr. Carter's evidence was therefore against Poisoning by arsenic being conclusively accepted as the cause of death, although subsequently he said he had no doubt it was arsenic.

Dr. Barron's evidence as to the cause of death was that he considered from the postmortem appearances that death was due to inflammation of the stomach and bowels, due to some irritant poison, but that he was unable to point to the particular poison, apart from what he heard; and, pressed as to what he meant by poison, the witness stated that poison might be bad tinned meat, bad fish, mussels, or generally bad food of any kind, or alcohol taken in excess.

The Chief Witness for the Prosecution

Dr. Stevenson expressed his opinion that the deceased died from arsenic poisoning, giving as his reasons that the main symptoms were those attributable to an irritant poison, and that they more closely resembled those of arsenic than of any other irritant of which he knew. He stated that he had known a great number of cases of poisoning by arsenic in every shape, and that he acted officially for the Home Office and Treasury in such cases. Dr. Stevenson was the witness of the prosecution, and gave his evidence before he had heard the evidence for the defense.

Dr. Stevenson also stated that the general symptoms of arsenic poisoning appeared within half an hour of taking some article of food or medicine, and were nausea, with a sinking sensation of the stomach; vomiting, which, unlike that produced by any ordinary article of food or drink that disagrees, afforded as a rule no relief and often came on again; that there was most commonly pain in the stomach, diarrhea; after a time the region of the stomach becomes tender under pressure, the patient becomes restless, often bathed in perspiration; the throat is complained of; pain in the throat, extending down to the stomach; the tongue becomes very foul in appearance and furred. There is not a bad smell as in the ordinary dyspeptic tongue, a rapid and feeble pulse, thirst, great straining at stool, vomits and evacuations frequently stained with blood. Of fourteen symptoms of arsenic poisoning named by Dr. Stevenson, Mr. Maybrick exhibited only one, according to the testimony of Dr. Stevenson. With the exception of the foul tongue with malodorous breath, none of these symptoms coincided with those given by Drs. Humphreys and Carter, who were in attendance on the patient, while Dr. Stevenson never saw him.

Medical Evidence for Defense

Then came the evidence for the defense, rebutting the presumption that death was caused by arsenic. First in order being Dr. Tidy, the examiner for forensic medicine at the London Hospital, and also, like Dr. Stevenson, employed as an analyst by the Home Office. This witness stated that, within a few years, close upon forty cases of arsenical poisoning had come before him, which enabled him to indicate the recurring and distinctive indications formed in such cases.

Dr. Tidy describes the symptoms of arsenic poisoning as purging and vomiting in a very excessive degree; a burning pain in the abdomen, more marked in the pit of the stomach, and increased considerably by pressure, usually associated with pain in the calves of the legs; then, after a certain interval, suffusion of the eyes—the eyes fill with tears; great irritability about the eyelids; frequent intolerance of light.

Dr. Tidy added that there were three symptoms, such as cramps, tenesmus, straining, more or less present, but the prominent symptoms were those he had mentioned, especially the sickness, violent, incessant sickness, and that poisoning by arsenic was extremely simple to detect. Further, that he (Dr. Tidy) had known cases where one or more of the four symptoms mentioned had been absent, but he had never known a case in which all four symptoms were absent; and stated that he had followed every detail of the Maybrick case so far as he could, and had read all the depositions before the coroner and magistrate, and the account of the vomiting did not agree with his description of excessive and persistent vomiting, and was certainly not that kind of vomiting that takes place in a typical case of arsenical poisoning.

Dr. Tidy further stated that, taking the whole of the symptoms, they undoubtedly were not those of arsenical poisoning, nor did they point to such, but were perfectly consistent with death from gastro-enteritis, not caused by arsenical poisoning at all; and that, had he been called upon to advise, he should have said it was undoubtedly not arsenical poisoning, and that his view had been very much strengthened, to use his own words, by the result of the post-mortem, which distinctly pointed away from arsenic.

Then there was the evidence, in the same direction, of Dr. Macnamara, the president of the Royal College of Surgeons, and its representative on the General Medical Council of the Kingdom, which is summed up in the general question put to him and his answer:

Question: Now, bringing your best judgment to bear on the matter—you having been present at the whole of this trial and heard the evidence—in your opinion, was this death from arsenical poisoning?

Answer: Certainly not.

In cross-examination Dr. Macnamara stated that, to the best of his judgment, Mr. Maybrick died of gastro-enteritis, not connected with arsenical poisoning, and which might have been caused by the wetting at the Wirrall races.

Dr. Paul, professor of medical jurisprudence at University College, Liverpool, and pathologist at the Royal Infirmary, stated he had made and assisted at something like three or four thousand post-mortem examinations, and that the symptoms in the present case agreed with cases of gastro-enteritis pitrc and simple; that the finding of the arsenic in the body, in the quantity mentioned in the evidence, was quite consistent with the case of a man who had taken arsenic medicinally, but who had lejt it off for some time, even for several months.

A Toxicological Study

So positive were Dr. Tidy and Dr. Macnamara of their position as to the effect of arsenic on the human system, that they subsequently published "A Toxicological Study of the Maybrick Case," thus challenging medical critics the world over to refute them. From this study the following, in tabular form, is taken, in order to contrast the symptoms from which Mr. Maybrick suffered with those which, it will be generally admitted, are the usual symptoms of arsenical poisoning: [table omitted]

"Maybrick's symptoms are as unlike poisoning by arsenic as it is possible for a case of dyspepsia to be. Everything distinctive of arsenic is absent. The urine contained no arsenic. The symptoms are not even consistent with arsenical poisoning.

"Regarding the treatment adopted by the medical men, and more especially Dr. Carter's action with regard to the meat juice, we are justified in assuming that the doctors themselves, even after a certain suggestion had been made to them, did not come to the conclusion that the illness of Maybrick was the result of arsenic.

"It is noteworthy (1) that none was found in the stomach; (2) that Maybrick was in the habit of taking drugs, and among them arsenic.

"Thus two conclusions are forced upon us:

"(1) That the arsenic found in Maybrick's body may have been taken in merely medicinal doses, and that probably it was so taken.

"(2) That the arsenic may have been taken a considerable time before either his death or illness, and that probably it was so taken.

"Our toxicological studies have led us to the three following conclusions:

"(1) That the symptoms from which Maybrick suffered are consistent with any form of acute dyspepsia, but that they point away from, rather than toward, arsenic as the cause of such dyspeptic condition.

"(2) That the post-mortem appearances are indicative of inflammation, but that they emphatically point away from arsenic as the cause of death.

"(3) That the analysis fails to find more than one-twentieth part of a fatal dose of arsenic, and that the quantity so found is perfectly consistent with its medicinal ingestion

The Medical Weakness of the Prosecution

Such was the complete evidence of the cause of death. The quantity of arsenic found in the body was one-tenth of a grain, and upon this evidence rests the first issue the jury had to consider, namely, whether it was proved beyond reasonable doubt that the deceased died from arsenical poisoning.

As to the value of the medical testimony on both sides, Dr. Humphreys admitted that he never attended a case of arsenical poisoning in his life, nor of any irritant poison, and that he would have given a certificate of death from natural causes had he not been told of arsenic found in the meat juice.

Dr. Carter laid no claim to any previous experience of poisoning by arsenic, and was unable to say from the post-mortem examination that arsenic was the cause of death, which he could only attribute to an irritant of some kind, and he admitted that it was the evidence of Mr. Davies, as to the finding of arsenic in the body, which led him to the conclusion that arsenical poisoning had taken place.

Dr. Barron did not see the patient, but assisted at the post-mortem examination, and stated that, judging by the appearances and apart from what he had heard, he was unable to identify arsenic as the particular poison which had set up the inflammation,

Now, assuming for a moment that this issue as to the cause of death rested entirely upon the uncontradicted testimony of these three doctors called for the prosecution, Humphreys, Carter, and Barron, the jury would not have been justified in coming to the conclusion that there was no reasonable doubt that arsenic poisoning was the cause of death. The doctors themselves had admitted that they were unable to arrive at that conclusion, apart from the evidence that arsenic was found in the body. The idea of arsenical poisoning never occurred to them from the symptoms, until the use of arsenic was first suggested.

The doctors could not say that death resulted from arsenic poisoning, and yet the jury have actually found that it did, in the face of the opinions of three eminent medical experts, who say it did not.

Even if these doctors had never been called at all for the defense, the jury were yet not justified in taking the evidence of Drs. Humphreys, Carter, and Barron, in the terms which they themselves never intended to pledge themselves to, namely, to exclude a reasonable doubt that death was due to arsenic.

Let us consider the position of the medical men called for the defense: Drs. Tidy, Macnamara, and Paul are the highest authorities on medical and chemical jurisprudence in Great Britain. No sort of hesitation or doubt attached to the opinions of any of them, and their experience of postmortem examinations was referred to, as including in the practise of Dr. Tidy, the Crown analyst, some forty cases of arsenic poisoning alone. Dr. Macnamara indorsed the opinion of Dr. Tidy. In addition to that, there was on the same side the evidence of Dr. Paul, professor of medical jurisprudence and toxicology at University College, Liverpool, with an experience of three or four thousand post-mortem examinations. It is impossible to conjecture by what process of reasoning the jury could have come to the conclusion, upon the evidence before them, that it was beyond a reasonable doubt that Mr. Maybrick had met his death by arsenical poisoning.

This volume of evidence before the jury pointed not only to a doubt as to the cause of death, but to a reasonable conclusion that it was not due to arsenical poisoning. It is inconceivable that the jury should have found as they did, except 'under the mandatory direction of the judge, which left them apparently no alternative but to substitute his opinions and judgment for their own, so that on that issue the finding was not so much the finding of the jury, to which the prisoner was by law entitled, but the finding of the judge, of whom the jury, abrogating their own functions, became the mere mouthpieces.

The Administration of Arsenic

The consideration of the facts as given in evidence also covers the second issue which the jury had to determine, namely, whether, if arsenic poisoning was the cause of death, it was the prisoner who administered it with criminal intent. The evidence on this point was most inconclusive.

No one saw the prisoner administer arsenic to her husband.

She had no opportunity of giving her husband anything since one or two o'clock on Wednesday afternoon (8th of May), after which she was closely watched by the nurses. It was not shown that any food or drink administered to the deceased by the prisoner contained arsenic. It was not shown that the prisoner had placed arsenic in any food or drink intended for her husband's use. Nor, in fact, was any found, although searched for, in any food or medicine of which Mr. Maybrick partook during his illness, except the arsenic in Fowler s solution, prescribed and administered by Dr. Humphreys himself.

The Fly-Paper Episode

The episode of the fly-papers may be considered as one of the most important factors in the whole case. It supplies, so to speak, the only link between Mrs. Maybrick and arsenic, which, it is well-known, forms their chief ingredient. It was proved she had purchased the fly-papers without any attempt at concealment, and, while soaking, they were exposed to everybody's view, quite openly, in a room accessible to every inmate of the house. It was not suggested that Mrs. Maybrick bought the other large quantity of arsenic, between seventy and eighty grains, found in the house after death, and no one came forward to speak to any such purchase. It was found in the most unlikely places for Mrs. Maybrick to have selected, if she had intended to use it, and the evidence against her on this point is of a particularly vague and indefinite character. [Justice Stephen, commenting on the quantity of arsenic found on the premises, himself observed that it was a remarkable fact in the case, and which, it appeared to him, told most favorably than otherwise for the prisoner, as in the whole case, from first to last, there was no evidence at all that she had bought any poison, or had anything to do with the procuring of any, with the exception of those fly-papers.] The accusation rests entirely on suspicion, insinuation, and circumstantial suggestions; not one tittle of evidence was adduced in support of it, and yet the jury came to the conclusion, without allowing of any doubt in the matter, that it was her hand which administered' the poison.

How Mrs. Maybrick Accounts for the Fly-Papers

On this question the prisoner made a statement. She accounted for the soaking of the fly-papers upon grounds which were not only probable, but were corroborated by other incidents. That she was in the habit of using arsenic as a face wash is shown by the prescription in 1878, before her marriage, and of which the chemist made an entry in his books, which came to light, after the trial, under the following circumstances:

Among the few articles which Mr. Maybrick's brothers allowed to be taken from the house, they being the legatees of the deceased, was a Bible which had belonged to Mrs. Maybrick's father, and which, with some other relics, came into the hands of Mrs. Maybrick's mother, the Baroness von Roques, who, months afterward, happening to turn over the leaves of the Bible, came across a small piece of printed paper, evidently mislaid there, being a New York chemist's label, with a New York doctor's prescription written on the back, for an arsenical face wash "for external use, to be applied with a sponge twice a day."

This prescription contained Fowler's solution of arsenic, chlorate of potash, rosewater, and rectified spirits; and was again made up, on the 17th of July, 1878, by a French chemist, Mr. L. Brouant, 81 Avenue D'Eylau, Paris. It corroborates Mrs. Maybrick's statement at the trial that the fly-papers were being soaked for the purpose alleged by her. If Mrs. Maybrick had obtained or purchased the seventy or eighty grains of arsenic found in the house after the death, it is inconceivable that she should have openly manufactured more arsenic with the fly-papers. At the time she prepared the statement she had reason to believe that the prescription had been lost. She knew, therefore, it would be impossible for her to corroborate her story about the face wash, and she could have omitted that incident altogether, and contented herself by saying that she learned the preparation while at school in Germany.

[In further explanation I desire to state that during my girlhood, as well as subsequently, I suffered occasionally, due to gastric causes, from an irritation of the skin. One of my schoolmates, observing that it troubled me a good deal, offered me a face lotion of her own preparation, explaining that it was much more difficult to obtain an arsenical ingredient abroad than in America, and to avoid any consequent annoyance she extracted the necessary small quantity of arsenic by the soaking of flypapers. I had never had occasion to do so myself, as I had a prescription from Dr. Bay; but when I discovered that I had mislaid or lost this, I recalled the method of my friend, being, however, wholly ignorant of what quantity might be required. The reason why I wanted a cosmetic at this time was that I was going to a fancy dress ball with my husband's brother, and that my face was at that time in an uncomfortable state of irritation.—F. E. M.]

Administration of Arsenic not Proved

Dealing with the question, did Mrs. Maybrick administer the arsenic, there is absolutely no evidence that she did. It was not for the prisoner to prove her innocence. She was seen neither to administer the arsenic nor to put it in the food or drink taken by the deceased, and this issue was found against her in the absence of any evidence in support.

Intent to Murder not Proved

Mrs. Maybrick's statement also bears strongly upon the question of administering with intent to murder. It is equally inconceivable that a guilty woman would have said anything about the white powder in the meat juice. She had nothing to gain by making such a statement, which could only land her in the sea of difficulties without any possible benefit, and here again the probabilities are entirely in her favor. It is beyond a doubt that Mr. Maybrick was in the habit, or had at some time or other been in the habit, of drugging himself with all sorts of medicines, including arsenic, and assumably he had obtained relief from it, or he would not have continued the practise.

Mr. Justice Stephen, in his summing-up, animadverted in very strong terms on the testimony of arsenic being used for cosmetic j)imposes, although expert chemists had certified to large use of arsenic for such a purpose. An immense degree of speculation must have entered the minds of the jury before they could find as they did, and bridge the gulf between the soaking of the fly-papers and the death of Mr. Maybrick, for it is quite evident that the soaking of the fly-papers was the one connection between the arsenic and the prisoner upon which all the subsequent events turned; and, if that be so, the importance is seen at once of the statement she made regarding that incident, and conclusive evidence as to which was subsequently found in the providentially recovered prescription.

Absence of Concealment by Prisoner

Another remarkable circumstance is the absence of any attempt at concealment on the prisoner's part. The fly-papers were purchased openly from chemists who knew the Maybricks well, and they were left soaking in such a manner as at once to refute any suggestion of secrecy; and her voluntary statement about the white powder which she placed in the meat juice, as to which there was absolutely no evidence to connect her with its presence there, seems inconsistent with the theory the prosecution attempted to build upon a number of assumptions of which the accuracy was not proved.

The question of the prisoner's guilt was not capable of being reduced to any issue upon which the prosecution could bring to bear direct evidence; the most they were capable of doing was to show that the prisoner had opportunities of administering poison, which she shared with every individual in the house; further, that she had arsenic in her possession (and this was an open secret, as we have already explained with reference to the fly-papers); and, lastly, that she had the possibility of extracting arsenic in sufficient quantities to cause death, which was, however, extremely doubtful; and then the prosecution tried to complete this indirect evidence by proving that Mr. Maybrick died from arsenic poisoning, which they signally failed to do. The strong point of the prosecution, as they alleged, was that a bottle of Valentine's meat juice had been seen in her hands on the night of Thursday, the 9th of May, and she replaced it in the bedroom, where it was afterward found by Michael Maybrick, and analyzed by Mr. Davis, who found half a grain of "arsenic in solution"; but there was no direct proof of such as is absolutely necessary to a conviction in a criminal case, of the identity of the bottle seen in Mrs. Maybrick's hands and that given to the analyst, and there was evidence that it had remained in the bedroom within reach of anybody, Mr. Maybrick himself included, for eighteen hours, and did not until the next day reach the hands of the analyst. These bottles are all alike in appearance, of similar turnip-like shape as the bovril bottles now sold, and it is clear there was more than one, because Dr. Humphreys says in his evidence that on visiting his patient on the 6th of May he found some of the Valentine's meat extract had made Mr. Maybrick sick, which he was not surprised at, as it often made people sick; while Nurse Gore, speaking of the bottle seen in the hands of Mrs. Maybrick, said it was a fresh, unused bottle, which she had herself opened only an hour before.

No evidence was given of what became of the opened bottle, and the presence of the arsenic having already been accounted for, and the fact recorded that the meat juice was not given to Mr. Maybrick, there is nothing to add to what has already been said, except that the account exactly dovetails with the prisoner's own voluntary statement.

Can anyone, closely following the evidence throughout, fail to be impressed with the inconsistency of Mrs. Maybrick's conduct in relation to her husband's illness with a desire to murder him? In all recorded cases of poisoning, the utmost precautions to screen the victim from observation have been observed. In the present instance it would seem as if just the reverse object had been aimed at. We find the prisoner first giving the alarm about the attack of illness; first sending for the doctors, brothers, and friends; first suggesting that something taken by her husband, some drug or medicine, was at the bottom of the mischief. We find the very first thing she does is to administer a mustard emetic—the last thing one would have expected if there had been a desire to poison him. If the prisoner had wished to put everybody in the house, and the doctors themselves, on the scent of poison, she could not have acted differently.

SOME IMPORTANT DEDUCTIONS

From Medical Testimony

FROM Dr. Humphreys' testimony it appears that, after the days when he was away from the patient, and when Mrs. Maybrick had undisturbed access to her husband, no symptoms whatever of arsenical poisoning appeared. If, then, arsenic was administered by Mrs. Maybrick under the doctors' eyes, without their detecting it, what value can attach to the testimony of the medical attendants as to the cause of death, apart from the post-mortem examination, by which they practically admit they allowed their judgment to be governed?

Does not the only alternative present itself that Drs. Humphreys and Carter are driven to the admission: "That the deceased died of arsenical poisoning we deduce, not from the symptoms during life, but from the fact that arsenic was found in the body after death"?

Symptoms Due to Poisonous Drugs

From the medical testimony it appears that the following' list of poisonous drugs was prescribed and administered to Mr. Maybrick shortly before his death:

April 28, 1899, diluted prussic acid; April 29, Papainc's iridin; May 3, morphia suppository; May 4, ipecacuanha; May 5, prussic acid; May 6, Fowler's solution of arsenic; May 7, jaborandi tincture and antipyrin; May 10, sulfonal, cocain, and phosphoric acid.

Also, during the same period, the following were prescribed: bismuth, double doses; nitro-glyccrin; cascara; nitro-hydro-chloric acid (composed of nux vomica, strychnin, and brucine); Plummer's pills (containing antimony and calomel); bromide of potassium; tincture of hyoscya-mus; tincture of henbane; chlorin.

Now it will be observed that up to May 6, when Fowler's solution of arsenic was administered, no symptom whatever had been observed at all compatible with the effects of arsenic.

The sickness produced by the morphia continued after the taking of arsenic, and down the unfortunate man's throat prussic acid, papaine, iridin, morphia, ipecacuanha, and arsenic, some of the most powerful drugs known to the pharmacopoeia, had found their way by the advice of Dr. Humphreys, in less than a week, while he was told to eat nothing, and allay his thirst with a damp cloth; and the charge of poisoning is made against the prisoner because he is suggested to have had an irritant poison in his stomach, and minute traces of arsenic in some other organs, within five days afterward.

Death from Natural Causes

The whole history of the case, from its medical aspect, is consistent with the small quantity of arsenic found in the body being part of that prescribed by Dr. Humphreys, or the remains of that taken by the deceased himself, there being no particle of evidence to show that he discontinued the habit of drugging himself almost up to the day of his death. This is also in accord with the evidence of Dr. Carter, who attended at a later period, and, taken as a whole, the evidence of both of these doctors, as well as their treatment of the deceased, points to death from natural causes.

Prosecution's Deductions from Postmortem Analysis Misleading

The evidence of the prosecution in connection with the analysis was thoroughly unreliable and misleading. Dr. Stevenson's difficulty was that, while two grains of arsenic was the smallest quantity capable of killing, the analyst had found only one-tenth of a grain, or the twentieth part of the smallest fatal dose, and, in substance, Dr. Stevenson proceeds to argue as follows:

(a) I found 0.015 grain of arsenic in 8 ounces of intestines. (There is no record as to what part of the intestines he examined.) I have weighed the intestines of some other person (not Mr. Maybrick), and find their entire weight to be so much. If, then, 8 ounces of Mr. Maybrick's intestines yield 0.015 grain, the entire intestines (calculated from the weight of someone else's intestines), had I analyzed them, would have yielded one-eleventh of a grain.

(b) Dr. Stevenson then proceeds to argue: "I found 0.026 grain of arsenic in 4 ounces of liver. The entire liver weighed 48 ounces, therefore the entire liver contained 0.32 grain of arsenic!'

{e} Dr. Stevenson argues further: "The intestines and liver, therefore, may be taken to contain together four-tenths of a grain of arsenic, and, having found four-tenths of a grain, I assume that the body at the time of death probably contained a fatal dose of arsenic!'

Such was the deduction Dr. Stevenson 361 arrived at, necessitating the assumption that arsenic was equally distributed m the intestines and liver, whereas it is within the personal knowledge of eminent men (such as Drs. Tidy and Macnamara) that arsenic may be found after death in one portion of the intestines, and not a trace of it in any other part. That in arsenical poisoning the arsenic may be found in the rectum and in the duodenum, and in no other part, is beyond dispute, and the fallacy of Dr. Stevenson's process must be self-evident.

The witnesses for the prosecution themselves supply the proof of the unequal distribution of the arsenic in the liver.

Mr. Davies calculates the quantity in the whole liver as 0.130 grain.

Dr. Stevenson, in his first experiment, puts it at 0.312 grain, and in his second experiment at 0.278 grain; in other words, Dr. Stevenson finds double in one experiment and considerably more than double in another experiment, the quantity found by Mr. Davies, and it is upon this glaring miscalculation and discrepancy that the ease for the prosecution was made to rest, and Mrs. Maybrick was convicted.

But with all this miscalculation the approximate amount of arsenic can only be swelled up to four-tenths of a grain, less than one-fourth of a fatal dose, and it was demonstrated that every other part of the body, urine, bile, stomach, contents of stomach, heart, lungs, spleen, fluid from mouth, and even bones, were all found to be free from arsenic.

Recapitulation of Legal Points

The legal points of the case may thus conveniently be recapitulated under the following short heads:

There was no conclusive evidence that Mr. Maybrick died from other than natural causes (the word "conclusive" being used in the sense of free from doubt).

There was no conclusive evidence that he died from arsenical poisoning.

There was no evidence that the prisoner administered or attempted to administer arsenic to him.

There was no evidence that the prisoner, if she did administer or attempt to administer arsenic, did so with intent to murder.

The judge, while engaged in his summing-up, placed himself in a position where his mind was open to the influence of public discussion and prejudice, to which was probably attributable the evident change in his summing-up between the first and second days; and he also *assumed facts against the prisoner which were not proved*.

The jury were allowed to separate and frequent places of public resort and entertainment during such summing-up.

The verdict was against the weight of evidence.

The jury did not give the prisoner the benefit of the doubt suggested by the disagreement of expert witnesses on a material issue in the case.

The Home Secretary should have remitted the entire sentence by reason of his being satisfied that there existed a reasonable doubt of her guilt, which, had it been taken into consideration at the time, would have entitled her to an acquittal.

The indictment contained no specific account of felonious administration of poison, and consequently the jury found the prisoner guilty of an offense for which she was never tried.

MRS. MAYBRICK'S OWN ANALYSIS

Of the Meat-juice Incident

I SAID in my statement to the Court, regarding this meat juice, that: "On Thursday night, the 9th, after Nurse Gore had given my husband beef juice, I went and sat on the bed by the side of him. He complained to me of feeling very sick, very weak, and very depressed, and again implored me to give him a powder, which he had referred to early in the evening and which I had then declined to give him. I was overwrought, terribly anxious, miserably unhappy, and his evident distress utterly unnerved me. He told me the powder would not harm him, and that I could put it in his food. I then consented. My lord, I had not one true or honest friend in the house. I had no one to consult and no one to advise me. I was deposed from my position as mistress in my own house and from the position of attending on my own husband, notwithstanding that he was so ill. Notwithstanding the evidence of nurses and servants, I may say that he wished to have me with him. [This desire was corroborated by the testimony of Nurse Callery.] He missed me whenever I was not with him. Whenever I went out of the room he asked for me, and for four days before he died I was not allowed to give him even a piece of ice without its being taken from my hand. When I found the powder I took it into the inner room, and in pushing through the door I upset the bottle, and, in order to make up the quantity of fluid spilled. I added a considerable quantity of water. On returning to the room I found my husband asleep, and I placed the bottle on the table by the window. When he awoke he had a choking sensation in his throat and vomiting. After that he appeared a little better. As he did not ask for the powder again, and as l was not anxious to give it to him, I removed the bottle from the small table, where it would attract his attention, to the top of the washstand, where he could not see it. There I left it until I believe Mr. Michael Maybrick took possession of it. Until a few minutes before Mr. Bryning made the terrible charge against me, no one in that house had informed me of the fact that a death certificate had been refused, or that a post-mortem examination had taken place, or that there was any reason to suppose that my husband died from other than natural causes. It was only when Mrs. Briggs alluded to the presence of arsenic in the meat juice that I was made aware of the [supposed] nature of the powder my husband had asked me to give him. I then attempted to make an explanation to Mrs. Briggs, such as I am now making to your lordship, when a policeman interrupted the conversation and put a stop to it."

Sometime after my conviction there was found among my effects a prescription for a face wash containing arsenic (the existence of which Justice Stephen in his summing up flouted as an invention of mine to cover an intent to poison). This, together with the fact that on analysis no trace of "fiber" was discovered in the body or in any of the things containing poison found in the house, should remove the "fly-paper incident" from all serious consideration in its bearing on the case (although it was the source of all "suspicions" before death).

There remain only as "circumstantial evidence of guilt" what has come to be known as the "motive," and the Valentine's meat-juice incident. The "motive," however regarded, was surely no incentive to murder, as inasmuch if I wanted to be free there was sufficient evidence in my possession (in the nature of infidelity and cruelty) to secure a divorce, and it was with regard to steps in that direction that I had already taken that I made confession to my husband after our reconciliation, and to which I referred as to the "wrong" I had done him, because of the publicity and ruin to his business it involved. The "motive," which was introduced into the case in the form of a letter written by me on the 8th of May, in which I said that my husband was "sick unto death," was made much of by the prosecution, and it led Justice Stephen to say, in his summing-up, "that I could not have known that my husband was dying (except I knew something others did not suspect), inasmuch as the doctors, from the diagnosis, did not consider the case at all serious." The justice either did not or would not understand (though it was testified to) that the phrase, "sick unto death," is an American colloquialism, especially of the South, and commonly employed with reference to any illness at all serious. Aside from the fact that all in attendance (save and except the doctors per their medical testimony) did regard it as serious—a witness for the prosecution, Mrs. Briggs, testified that she regarded him on that day as "dangerously ill," and Mr. Michael Maybrick said that when he saw his brother on the evening of the same day "he was shocked by his appearance"—I may say here that the phrase "sick unto death," in connection with other causes for apprehension, was prompted by the fact that my husband had told me that very morning that "he thought he was going to die"; and that this was his feeling is conclusively shown by the evidence of I)r. Humphreys at the inquest, when he testified that he had remarked to Mr. Michael Maybrick on this same Wednesday, the 8th of May: " I am not satisfied with your brother, and I will tell you why [not because the symptoms seemed serious to him, it will be observed]. Your brother tells me he is going to die!'

That I regarded the case as really serious is surely further supported by the fact that, notwithstanding the easy-going attitude of Dr. Humphreys, I had persisted in urging a consultation, which accordingly took place on the 7th. As to what the attending physicians knew or did not know about the medical aspects of the case, I confidently refer the reader to their own remarkable testimony.

There then remains for serious consideration only what is known as the "Valentine meat-juice incident." Of this I know no more now than is included in my statement at the trial—namely, that at my husband's urgent, piteous request I placed a powder (which by his direction I took from a pocket in his vest, hanging in the adjoining room, which room until his sickness had been his private bedroom, he having been removed to mine as being larger and more airy) in a bottle of meat juice, no part of the contents of which were given him, and hence at the very most there could only have legally arisen from this act a charge of "intent to poison."

I do not assume that I can solve a problem that has puzzled so many able minds, but I trust I shall make clear that the prosecution cannot acquit itself of the inference of "cooking" up a case against me with reference to this meat-juice incident: i. At the inquest, only a few days after 37i the occurrence, Nurse Gore testified, "I could and did see clearly what Mrs. Maybrick did with the bottle," though she failed to tell what she saw; and it is remarkable she was not further questioned on this point. At the magisterial inquiry and trial, per contra, she testified that "she [I] pushed the door to conceal (note the animus) her [my] movements"; but on cross-examination she so far corrected herself as to say: "Mrs. Maybrick did not shut the dressing-room door."

2. When I returned with the bottle to the sick-room, she testified that I placed it on the table in a "surreptitious manner," though this action, according to her own testimony, happened while "she [I] raised her right hand and replaced the bottle on the table, while she [I] was talking to me [her]."

If one wanted to do such an act "surreptitiously," would one choose the moment of all others when by conversation one is calling attention to oneself? Do not the two things involve a direct contradiction?

3. It is in evidence that an hour after I had placed the bottle on a little table in the window, I returned to the room and removed it from the table to the washstand (where it remained during most of the next day), lest the sight of it should renew Mr. Maybrick's desire for it, as he had just awakened. Note how this bottle is juggled with by the witnesses for the prosecution.

Michael Maybrick, at the inquest, in answer to the question, "Where did you find the Valentine's meat juice?" replied: "I found it on a little table mixed-up with several other bottles." Note the particularity of this bottle being mixed up with several other bottles. Obviously he at this time, only a few days after the event, had a clear picture of the situation in his mind. In corroboration of this testimony that the bottle he took was on the table and not on the washstand, there is the testimony of Nurse Callery, who at the inquest stated: "My attention was called by her [Nurse Gore] to a bottle of Valentine's meat juice, which was on a table in Mr. Maybrick's room. I took a sample. I don't know what became of the bottle of meat juice. I saw Mr. Michael Maybrick in the room before going off duty at 4.50 p.m on Friday, but did not see him take the meat juice away."

Nurse Gore gave her testimony at the inquest after the two others, and deposed that Mr. Michael Maybrick took the bottle from the washstand where I had placed it, thus contradicting Michael Maybrick, and in a way also Nurse Callery, who testified that Nurse Gore called her attention to a bottle on the small table. Obviously this difference introduces *two* bottles; but this would never answer the prosecution, and accordingly Mr. Michael Maybrick at the trial dropped the table sworn to at the inquest and fell in line with Nurse Gore in so far as to say: "It was standing on the washstand, and it was among some other bottles'.' Note that, while he substitutes the washstand for the table, he still clings to the bottles—a most important circumstance—as it was indubitably shown that there were on the washstand only the "ordinary basins and jugs" (water pitchers). Obviously Mr. Michael Maybrick had not fully comprehended the purpose of the prosecution in "harmonizing" the testimony with that of Nurse Gore; the "bottles" were too clearly in his mind to be dropped without a distinct effort, and he naturally introduced them again; and, to fit in with the Nurse Gore and the amended Mr. Michael Maybrick evidence, Nurse Callery also changed front at the trial, and the table of her inquest testimony is also turned into a washstand. It is in evidence that as late as the 6th of May my husband took meat juice out of a bottle then in the room, the contents of which, however, did not agree with him, and upon the order of Dr. Humphreys its giving was discontinued, he adding that he was "not surprised," as it was known not to agree with some people.

Although this was the doctors order, Mr. Edwin Maybrick took it upon himself to procure a fresh bottle, and, distinctly against the same order, Nurse Gore set about to administer its contents. Subsequently a bottle of meat juice, half full, was found in a small wooden box with other bottles (one of them containing arsenic in solution) in my husband's hat-box.

Nevertheless, though we are here undeniably dealing with three meat-juice bottles, only two were accounted for at the trial. What became of the third bottle? And which of the three was missing? Now, furthermore, it is in evidence that Nurse Callery handled one of these bottles (between the time that I placed one on the washstand and the time when Mr. Michael Maybrick, more than twelve hours later, took one either from the table or the wash-stand for analysis), for she took a sample of it, which she afterward threw away.

As all Valentine's meat-juice bottles look alike, Mr. Michael Maybrick showed sufficient caution to say he could not identify the bottle shown him; but Nurse Gore, to whom every act of mine, however innocent, was fraught with "surreptitiousness" and "suspicion," balked at no such scruples, but boldly testified that the bottle produced in court was the identical one that Mr. Michael Maybrick "took from the washstand," even though at the inquest, when his memory was freshest, he testified that he took it from the table.

It should be remembered that my statement to the court was to the effect that I put a powder (its nature unknown to me) in the meat-juice bottle I had in my hands. Yet no bottle containing a powder, or in which a powder had been dissolved, appeared in evidence. According to the analyst, the bottle submitted to him contained arsenic that had been put in in a state of solution. Now it resolves itself to this: either I uttered a falsehood about the powder and really introduced a solution, or another bottle was substituted for the one I had for two minutes in my possession.

The contention of the prosecution was that I "invented" the powder, precisely as it was contended I "invented" the face-wash prescription which was found after the trial. If I "invented" the powder, how did I come by the solution? If I had had arsenic in solution in my possession, would I have gone to the trouble of making a solution for a face wash by the clumsy method of soaking fly-papers? Is not the proposition quite absurd on its face—that I should openly call attention to a method of arsenic extraction with the object of murder, when I already had the means at my command?

Finally, let it be borne in mind, as stated by Justice Stephen himself as a remarkable fact, that no arsenic was traced to my procurement or found in my personal belongings (save and except the innocuous flypapers), and I may add that no arsenic was traced to anyone connected with the case, except to my husband.

I say it is absolutely clear that the bottle of Valentine's meat juice which Mr. Michael Maybrick took possession of and handed to Dr. Carter is not the same bottle which Nurse Gore saw me place on the washstand. There should be no flaw in the identity of the bottle which was handed to the analyst and the one which was in my hands, and I think the reader will say that it is impossible to conceive a greater flaw in any evidence of identity than shown by these witnesses of the prosecution at the inquest, when their minds were freshest as to their respective parts in this incident, and at the trial.

Those of my readers who follow the analysis of the testimony as presented by Messrs. Lumley & Lumley can hardly have failed to be impressed by the fact that I was surrounded by unscrupulous enemies, by people who not only had extraordinary knowledge as to where to look for deposits of arsenic, but also remarkable intuitions that arsenic had been administered before any evidence of the presence of poison had been analytically proven.

In the above I have not aimed to make an analysis of the testimony, such as, for example, on the evidence now available, Lord Russell could have made; I have simply endeavored to satisfy my readers that I have substantial grounds for asserting my innocence before the world.

Florence Elizabeth Maybrick.

MEMORIALS FOR RESPITE OF SENTENCE

From the Physicians of Liverpool

IN a memorial for respite of sentence of Mrs. Maybrick, which was signed by leading medical practitioners of Liverpool, the petitioners say in part:

"3. It was admitted by the medical testimony on behalf of the prosecution that the symptoms during life and the post-mortem appearances were in themselves insufficient to justify the conclusion that death was caused by arsenic, and that it was only the discovery of traces of that poison in certain parts of the viscera which eventually led to that conclusion.

"4. The arsenic so found in the viscera was less in quantity than that found in any previous case of arsenical poisoning in which arsenic has been found, at all.

"5. There was indisputable evidence on the part of the defense that the deceased had been in the habit of taking arsenic, both medicinally and otherwise, for many years, and that the small quantity found in the viscera was inconsistent with the theory of a fatal dose at any time or times during the period covered by the illness of the deceased.

"6. Lastly, your memorialists agree with the evidence given by Dr. Tidy, Dr. Macnamara, and Mr. Paul on behalf of the defense, that the medical evidence on behalf of the prosecution had entirely failed to prove that the death was due to arsenical poisoning at all?

From the Bars of Liverpool and London

Leading members of the Bars of Liverpool and London signed a memorial praying a reprieve of Mrs. Maybrick's sentence "on the ground... of the great conflict of medical testimony as to the cause of death" of Mr. Maybrick.

From Citizens of Liverpool

A petition for reprieve of Mrs. Maybrick's sentence was signed by many and influential citizens of Liverpool. Among the reasons urged were:

3. Lack of direct evidence of administration of arsenic.

4. The weak case against prisoner on general facts unduly prejudiced by evidence of motive.

5. Preponderance of medical testimony that death was ascribable to natural causes.

[I feel a deep respect for the noble avowal given in the petition of the medical practitioners of Liverpool, who must have felt the honor of their profession at stake, and that their individual dignity and humanity were concerned. The feeling among the Bar on receipt of the verdict was an almost universal, if not a quite unanimous, one of surprise. I have already mentioned (in Part One, the change of attitude of the citizens of Liverpool toward me, as the trial progressed, from hostility to belief in my innocence. F. E. M.]

NEW EVIDENCE

Arsenic Sold to Maybrick by Druggist

MR. EDWIN GARNETT HEATON, a retired chemist (druggist), formerly carried on business at 14 Exchange Street East, Liverpool, for seventeen years; he retired from business in 1888. He testified at the trial:

"Mr. Maybrick called frequently at my shop for about ten years or more, off and on. He used to get the tonic called 'pick-me-up.' He would come to the shop, get it, and drink it up. He gave me a prescription which altered it, which I put up with liquor arsenicalis. He brought the prescription for the first few times; I used afterward to give it him at once, when he came into the shop and gave his order. I prepared the c pick-me-up' and added the stuff. At the beginning of giving it to him, a certain quantity of liquor arsenicalis was given, and as it continued it was gradually increased from first to last, so at the last it was 75 per cent, greater in quantity than it was originally. He used to get it from two to five times a day, and each containing 75 per cent, increase."

This testimony of Mr. Heaton's was challenged by the prosecution, and considerably nullified by the fact that he did not know Mr. Maybrick, his customer, by name, but identified him by a photograph. To show how inexorably one fatality after another was woven into the web of my tragic case, it is in order to state that Mr. Heaton's connection with Mr. Maybrick could and would undoubtedly have been perfectly established but for what in the circumstances can be characterized only as a criminal blunder on the part of the police. In the printed police list of the score or more medicine bottles found locked in the private desk of Mr. Maybrick at his office was one entered as follows: "Spirit of salvolatile, Edwin G. Easton, Exchange Street-East, Liverpool." This misprint of Easton for Heaton escaped the attention of everybody at the trial, and thus prevented the defense from identifying most circumstantially Mr. Maybrick with Mr. Heaton's customer who had the arsenic habit.

Arsenic Supplied to Maybrick by Manufacturing Chemist

About ten years ago Mr. Valentine Charles Blake, of Victoria Embankment, son of a well-known baronet and Member of Parliament, made a voluntary statutory declaration [corroborated on oath in every possible essential by William Bryer Nation, of No. 7 Lion Street, a manufacturing chemist and patentee], that Mr. Maybrick, about two months before his death, procured through him (Mr. Blake), from Mr. Nation's supplies, as much as 150 grains of arsenic in various forms. Mr. Nation, assisted by Mr. Blake, had made certain chemical experiments in preparing ramie, the fiber of rhea grass, to serve as a substitute for cotton. Among other ingredients used was arsenic, some in pure form (white arsenic), some mixed with soot, and some mixed with charcoal. In January, 1889, the process was perfected, and sometime during the same month Mr. Nation sent Mr. Blake to see Mr. Maybrick, to get his assistance in placing the product on the market. Mr. Maybrick was interested in the proposition and inquired closely into the nature of the process, what ingredients were used, etc. The deponent told him that, among other materials, arsenic was employed.

Then, to quote the exact words of the deposition, Mr. Blake went on to say:

"14. The said Mr. Maybrick shortly afterward, during discussion at the same interview, asked me whether I had heard that many inhabitants of Styria, in Austria, habitually took arsenic internally and throve upon it. I said that I had heard so.

He then spoke to me of De Quincey, the author of 'Confessions of an Opium-Eater,' and asked me had I read the work. I said, 'Yes,' and that I wondered De Quincey could have taken such a quantity as 900 drops of laudanum in a day. The said James Maybrick said, 'One man's poison is another man's meat, and there is a so-called poison which is like meat and liquor to me whenever I feel weak and depressed. It makes me stronger in mind and in body at once,' or words to that effect. I ventured to ask him what it was. He answered, 'I don't tell everybody, and wouldn't tell you, only you mentioned arsenic. It is arsenic. I take it when I can get it, but the doctors won't put any into my medicine except now and then a trifle, that only tantalizes me,' or words to that effect. After a pause, during which I said nothing, the said James Maybrick said: 'Since you use arsenic, can you let me have some? I find a difficulty in getting it here.' I answered that I had some by me, and that, since I had only used it for experiments which were now perfected, I had no further use for it, and he (Maybrick) was welcome to all I had left. He then asked me what it was worth, and offered to pay for it in advance. I replied that I had no license to sell drugs, and suggested that we should make it a quid pro quo. Mr. Maybrick was to do his best with the ramie grass product, and I was to make him a present of the arsenic I had.

"15. It was finally agreed that when I came to Liverpool again, as arranged I should bring with me and hand him the arsenic aforesaid.

"16. In February, 1889, I again called at the office of the said James Maybrick, in Liverpool, and, as promised, I handed him all the arsenic I had at my command, amounting to about 150 grains, some of the 'white' and some of the two kinds of 'black' arsenic, in three separate paper packets. I told him to be careful, as he had almost enough to poison a regiment.' When we separated the said James Maybrick took away the said arsenic with him, saying he was going home to his house at Aigburth, to which he invited me. Having a train to catch, I declined the invitation, promising to accept it on my next visit to Liverpool, but before that occurred I read of his death.

"17. After the wife of the said James Maybrick had been accused of his alleged murder, I wrote to Mr. Cleaver, her then solicitor, of Liverpool, to the effect that I could give some evidence which might be of use to his client, and I posted such letter but received no reply.

"18. At this time I was intensely anxious as to the fate of my only son, Valentine Blake, who had in the previous year sailed on board the ship Melanasia from South Shields for Valparaiso, which ship was then very long overdue and unheard of. I eventually learned, as a result of a Board of Trade inquiry, that the said ship must have foundered with all hands, my only son included. At the time I wrote as aforesaid to Mr. Cleaver, my entire attention was engrossed in endeavoring to get news as to the ship which never came home, and

I felt little interest in any other subject. Receiving no reply to my said letter to Mr. Cleaver, I took no further steps in the matter until, seeing recently in a newspaper that Mr. Jonathan E. Harris, of 95 Leadenhall Street, in the city of London, was now acting for Mrs. James Maybrick and her mother, the Baroness de Roques, I called at the offices of the said Mr. Harris and made to him a statement."

Depositions as to Mr. Maybrick's Arsenic Habit

On August 10, Henry Bliss, former proprietor of Sefton Club and Chambers, Liverpool, made a sworn deposition, in which he said:

"Mr. Maybrick lived in the chambers on and off several months, and was in the habit of dosing himself. On one occasion he asked me to leave a prescription at a well-known Liverpool chemist's to be made up by the time he left 'Change. The chemist remarked: 'He ought to be very careful and not take an overdose of it.'

On March 31, 1891, Franklin George Bancroft, artist and writer, of Columbia, S. C., made a sworn deposition, in which he said:

"1. Between the years 1874 and 1876 I was personally acquainted with James Maybrick, late of Battlecrease House, Aigburth, near Liverpool, merchant, deceased, who was then living in Norfolk, Va. I was frequently in his company, and from time to time I have seen him fake from his vest pocket a case resembling a cigarette case, which contained a pa elect of white powders, and place the contents of one such powder on several occasions into the glass of wine (usually Chablis, claret, or champagne) he was at the time drinking, and swallow the same.

"2. Seeing him take this powder, I did, on one occasion, ask him what it was, and the said James Maybrick replied, 'Longevity and fair complexion, my boy!' and be subsequently informed me that the said white powders were composed of arsenic among other ingredients."

JUSTICE STEPHEN'S RETIREMENT

There are also facts in relation to the judge who tried the case which, had they been anticipated at the time of the trial, could not have failed to have had some weight, directly or indirectly, on the minds of the jury; that is to say, his retirement from the Bench not long afterward, in April, 1891, when, to quote his own words in addressing the Bar, of whom he was taking leave, "he had been made acquainted with the fact that he was regarded by some as no longer physically capable of discharging his duties"; and it will be no matter of surprise, to those who have read critically the summing-up of Mr. Justice Stephen on this trial, to notice the entire change from a favorable bias between his address to the jury on the first days of the trial to the violent hostility shown at its conclusion.

This change of front can be in a manner accounted for, as it had been suggested to the prisoner's friends, by a conversation on the case between Mr. Justice Stephen and another member of the Bench, Mr. Justice Grantham, at a social meeting of an entirely private character.

A mental malady was developed in the judge so soon after the trial that it was properly said to have been caused by his brooding over it, and this condition increased so rapidly and markedly that his resignation was demanded. It is but reasonable to suppose that the judge's mental incapacity reached farther back than its discovery, and that the illogical and unjust summing-up was connected with the mental overthrow of the otherwise able judge. And it maybe here added that Justice Stephen himself, in the second edition of the "General Views of the Criminal Law of England, 1890," says, at page 173, that out of 979 cases tried before him, from January, 1885, to September, 1889, "the case of Mrs. Maybrick was the only case in which there could be any doubt about the facts."

THE END

BIG BYTE BOOKS is your source for great lost history!

Printed in Great Britain
by Amazon